Living the Scriptures

Also by Mother Angelica:

Praying with Mother Angelica
Meditations on the Rosary, the Way of the
Cross, and Other Prayers

Mother Angelica on Christ and Our Lady

Mother Angelica on Suffering and Burnout

Mother Angelica's Quick Guide to the Sacraments

Mother Angelica on Prayer and Living for the Kingdom

Mother Angelica on God, His Home, and His Angels

Mother Angelica's Practical Guide to Holiness

Mother Angelica's Answers, Not Promises

A Holy Hour with Mother Angelica

Mother M. Angelica

Living the Scriptures

Edited by Daniel Hopkins

EWTN PUBLISHING, INC.
Irondale, Alabama

EWTN Publishing, Inc.
5817 Old Leeds Road, Irondale, AL 35210

Distributed by Sophia Institute Press, Box 5284, Manchester, NH 03108.

paperback ISBN 978-1-68278-238-5
ebook ISBN 978-1-68278-239-2
Library of Congress Control Number: 2021938705

First printing

In the beginning was the Word:
and the Word was with God
and the Word was God.
All that came to be had life in Him
and that life was the light of men,
a light that shines in the dark,
a light that darkness could not overpower.

—John 1:1–5

Your word is a lamp to my feet,
a light on my path.

—Psalm 119:105

Contents

1. Telling God We're Sorry 3

2. The Armor of God 11

3. Jesus and the Woman at the Well 21

4. Seeing Jesus with the Eyes of Faith 31

5. Learning from Jesus' Example 41

6. Casting Out a Demon 51

7. A Meal at a Pharisee's House 59

8. Putting God First 67

9. Jesus Feeds the Five Thousand and Walks on Water . . . 75

10. Jesus Heals a Demoniac 85

11. Jesus and the Syrophoenician Woman 93

12. Without Perception 101

13. The Gratitude of the Leper 109

14. The Witness of John the Baptist 119

15. St. John the Baptist's Commitment to Truth 129

16. The Raising of Lazarus 139

    Mother M. Angelica 149

Living the Scriptures

1

Telling God We're Sorry

Matthew 26

We're going to look at St. Matthew's Gospel. St. Matthew is an apostle who gives us great courage and strength, because he speaks so much of the mercy of God and the compassion of Jesus for poor sinners. We are all in that boat of having to look at God and say, "I'm sorry." We do that many times a day, and we get discouraged; we're just disheartened because we feel, "How many times do I have to say, 'I'm sorry'?" We wonder how many times we are going to fall into these imperfections or these sins or these realities. How many times? We just get disheartened, and we say, "Well, it's not worth it." It's a constant struggle. You think you've got it made, you think you have conquered something, and, all of a sudden, some temptation comes along, something hidden comes along, and down you go.

Well, if you have ever been in that kind of discouraging position, the Gospel of Matthew gives us courage. There are many, many examples of how Jesus treated real, true, sincere sinners. The people that Jesus was very, very hard on were the Pharisees, those proud people who really didn't commit too many sins, as far as the commandments were concerned. They kept the commandments, but they had pride and arrogance. They looked down on people and lorded over everyone. They were so justified in their own eyes

3

that they never needed repentance, never felt they needed to say to God, "I'm sorry." And so Jesus was very hard, but He was very compassionate.

Now, He didn't give us a lot of leeway. In today's world, we just think all we need is to say to Jesus, "I'm sorry" and then continue on in a sinful life. That's presumption. It means I presume upon God's mercy. It is an act of pride, because what we're saying to the Lord is, "Look. You are compassionate, so I can sin all I want, and then I will ask for mercy, and You will be merciful." And that's presumption. When we talk about sinners, we are talking about people who have their weaknesses and their "sinner condition," and they rise and they fall, but they are really and truly repentant. They are really repentant, and they have every determination that they shall not do this again.

Then there comes a time in our lives when perhaps we really do fall. It's those times when you think you have fallen so far that God cannot forgive you, when you think your sin is greater than His mercy. We call that the sin against the Holy Spirit. Why? Because if you think that your sins are greater than God's mercy, then you don't ask for forgiveness, and that leads to a condition, an attitude of pride. It looks like repentance, but it's remorse instead. That's what Judas had—remorse.

To give ourselves a little courage, there is in the twenty-sixth chapter of St. Matthew's Gospel a marvelous example of two different kinds of sorrow for sin. Turn to Matthew 26:69. This is when the Lord had been captured in the Garden of Olives, and He had gone before the Sanhedrin, and He was being tried. Peter followed Him, though at a distance. Peter was sitting outside in the courtyard, in fact, and the Scripture says, "a servant-girl came up to him and said, 'You too were with Jesus the Galilean.' But he denied it."

He denied it in front of everybody. What does that mean, "he denied it"? What it means is that Peter said, "I was not with Jesus of Nazareth." You see what fear did to Peter? His emotions were out of control. He had grief in his heart over the terrible reality that one of their own had denied Jesus, and there He was before the Sanhedrin, about to be condemned by an unjust people. Peter was frightened. Whom did he think of? Jesus? No, he thought of himself, as most of us do. "'I do not know what you are talking about,' he said. When he went out to the gate, another servant-girl saw him and said to the people all around, 'This man was with Jesus the Nazarene'. And again"—ah, but now his emotions are coming up to a fever pitch, and he takes an oath! —"with an oath, he denied it, 'I do not know the man'" (vv. 70–72).

It's hard to believe a man like Peter would do that. Can you kind of recall Peter, the man who said, "Thou art the Christ, the Son of the Living God" (see Matt. 16:16), the great fisherman who walked on the water? And yet here he is, after having seen miracle upon miracle, the dead rising, the lame walking, the deaf hearing, and the blind seeing, saying, "I don't know this Man."

Can't you just feel the hurt? Have you ever been hurt that way? I think everybody has at one time or another had a dear, dear friend. Something happens to you where you need a shoulder to cry on or you need confirmation, assurance, or you need defense, and that friend turns around as if he never knew you. I don't think there's any hurt in the whole world that can compare with being terribly crushed by a dear, dear friend. It's really bad. "A little later the bystanders came up and said to Peter, 'You are one of them for sure! Why, your accent gives you away'" (v. 73).

So, again, the girl says, "Your accent gives you away." You know, we don't always think of Peter as having an accent, but he had a Galilean accent. It was rather peasant. It was not the best, and that's one of the beauties of Jesus. There are many, many beauties. And one is that He did not disdain being called "the Galilean."

Now Peter is really scared; he's running, and he curses. Not only that, but he calls down curses upon himself. I don't know what kind of curses they had in those days, like "May fire fall from heaven upon me," or "May lightning strike me dead." We've heard little things like that. I mean, he was frightened. He made an oath. He was scared stiff. All the time though, you see he is really going down. And the moment he took that oath and said for the third time, "I do not know the Man," the cock crew, and Peter remembered something. And when he remembered Jesus — that's important to really look at now. If you're following along in Scripture, look at that last sentence in this chapter: "And the Lord turned and looked straight at Peter, and Peter remembered what the Lord had said to him, 'Before the cock crows today, you will have disowned me three times.' And he went outside and wept bitterly" (Luke 22:61–62). Peter was very repentant.

That's a kind of clue for you and me, isn't it? We shouldn't let ourselves go as far down as Peter did. It should be that in the very beginning of a temptation, at the very beginning of something that wants us to hate someone or not forgive him, we should turn to Christ. We tend to think, "Well, So-and-so really hurt me. He really was unjust. He really cheated me." And so we use human truth to give ourselves the excuse of sinning. When we do that, it becomes very hard to resist the temptation.

And Peter felt in his heart, as he was denying the Lord once, twice, three times, he had in his heart that he was defending himself. He had a right to save his own life. Obviously, Jesus was out of his hands; there was nothing he could do. He hadn't listened when Jesus said, "I must go to Jerusalem and be crowned with thorns and scourged and crucified." He hadn't heard it. He didn't *want* to hear it! In fact, at one point he drew the Lord aside and he said, "Hey, wait a minute! If you want to go to Jerusalem, and all these things are going to happen to you, forget it. Don't go!"

Jesus said, "Get behind me, Satan!" (Matt. 16:23). Jesus called Peter a devil. I think that you and I get into that same position when we don't remember Jesus. Peter remembered Jesus, and he remembered what He said.

I know what some of you are thinking. You say, "Well, I never saw Jesus. After all, I didn't live with Jesus for three years." Oh, but you have seen Jesus. You *know* Jesus. If you're a Christian, you should know your Savior. You should know Jesus because He has saved you. He loves you. Everything good that happens to you comes from Him — *everything!* And even those things that are not so good are permitted for a greater good. The Lord must permit many things in our lives because we are all victims of other peoples' bad choices and sometimes our own. Jesus takes advantage of those occasions to make us patient and humble and to help us grow in faith, hope, and love. In the midst of great tragedies, many times great suffering, God brings beautiful jewels and treasures.

Luke 22:62 tells us something important: "And he went outside and wept bitterly." Now we have another sinner who did almost similar to Jesus as Judas. It says in Matthew 27:3–4, "When he found that Jesus had been condemned, Judas his betrayer was filled with remorse and took the thirty silver pieces back to the chief priests and elders. 'I have sinned,' he said. 'I have betrayed innocent blood.'" He knew it. "I have betrayed innocent blood." And do you know what the priests said? "What is that to us? That is your concern" (Matt. 27:4).

Has anyone ever gotten you into a problem? Some of you young girls were betrayed by your boyfriends, because you made a mistake and are now pregnant. You go to this young man who you thought loved you, and whom you love, and he just looks at you and says, "Hey, that's your problem." There are many of you out there who have had this kind of hurt, and it's a terrible thing.

Well, Judas couldn't take it, because he did not remember Jesus. He did not recall the merciful Jesus, Who forgave an adulteress, Who forgave Matthew, Who must have forgiven Judas himself many times. I personally think Judas was a character. He was a thief, a man who was constantly complaining about the money and where it was going and why they weren't keeping more—always mundane, always had money on his mind! And so Judas flung those thirty pieces of silver at the Temple steps, and he ran. Well, he ran and hanged himself.

What's the difference between Peter and Judas? The difference is vast: Peter was repentant, and Judas was remorseful. You say, "Well, what's the difference?" If you read this carefully, you will see the difference.

Repentance remembers love and repents not so much over the sin it committed but over the fact that it has offended a gentle, loving, compassionate God. Peter repents at the thought of having offended Jesus, that wonderful God-Man, Who forgave Peter, Who gave him the keys of the Kingdom and said, "So I now say to you: You are Peter and on this rock I will build my Church" (Matt. 16:18).

Judas, now, was remorseful. He knew he had sinned, but so had Peter. He knew he had betrayed innocent blood, and so did Peter. But Judas went out and hanged himself. It never dawned on Judas that the mercy and compassion of Jesus were greater than his sin. It did dawn on Peter, but Judas was not convinced of the divinity of Christ. And so he looked at a Man Whom he had denied, Whom he had betrayed, and said, "I have betrayed an innocent man."

Peter knew Who Jesus was. He didn't forget. I can imagine Peter sitting in the corner of some cave, weeping bitterly and saying, "Oh, God, I am so sorry. I was so weak. Jesus deserves so much more," and crying and crying because he had offended Jesus.

Luke's Gospel says that at that moment he denied Christ and the cock crew, it dawned on Peter what he had done. Luke says, "And the Lord turned and looked straight at Peter. . . . And he [Peter] went outside and wept bitterly" (22:61–62).

Can you imagine the hurt but compassionate eyes of Jesus? Can you imagine Jesus looking at Peter? Oh! We can't hardly imagine that. That's why, you see, there is such a difference between Peter and Judas. Judas committed suicide because he would not face his Lord and say, "I am sorry." It is a sin against the Holy Spirit to refuse to say to the One you offended—to Jesus, to the Father, to the Spirit—"I'm sorry." That's all it takes! It's not a big deal. It's to acknowledge our sin and to say, "I'm sorry."

One of the greatest evils today is that so many people are telling you, "This is not a sin," and "That is not a sin," and "All of these things are not sins. You just have to love." But love and sin don't go together! You cannot slap someone in the face and say, "I love you." That's ridiculous! But we slap God in the face when we sin, and we have big sins today—fornication, immorality, adultery. It's unbelievable what people do today under the guise of God's compassion. They've got misdirected faith or no faith at all.

How would you like it if your husband or wife came up to you, slapped you across the face, and said, "I love you"? That's the essence of sin, and it's a lie.

And so Peter acknowledged his sin and said, "I'm sorry." Judas said, "I have sinned against an innocent man." He lost sight of the divinity of Jesus, and he was not repentant; he was remorseful. He said, "I've got to get away from this thing!" It never dawned on him, and if it did, he thought that his sin was greater than God's mercy.

No one can forgive another person if that person never says, "I'm sorry." There's no way, no way at all. You cannot if a person is not at all repentant. And that has happened to you, I'm sure. Somebody has hurt you deeply, and you go up to him and say, "I'm very hurt over this."

He replies, "Well, I didn't do anything."

"I'm very hurt," you insist.

"Well, that's your problem."

Do you understand? We understand things on a human level, especially as far as we are concerned. But when it comes to our relationship with God, we kind of take away that experience, and we look at God and say, "Well, you've got to forgive me."

We need courage today to say, "I'm sorry." Don't be like Judas. Don't get discouraged, so remorseful, that you will not say to Jesus, "I'm sorry." I don't care what sins you have committed. The greatest thing Judas did was to deny the Lord's mercy and forgiveness. Can you imagine what the world would be like if we could say that Judas was forgiven by God? No one would ever, ever become disheartened. But he denied that glory to God by committing suicide and saying, "God cannot forgive me." So don't be like him.

Whatever you're doing that's sinful, repent. Change your life. Turn it over to the Lord. Say, "Lord, I am not going to commit this sin again. Your grace is greater than my weakness." And no matter what it is, He will forgive you. Just say, "I am sorry, Lord Jesus." A flood of mercy will come upon you, as it did Peter, because at the moment you say, "I am sorry," the eyes of Jesus look into your soul. And at that moment, that beautiful strength will return to you.

If you're Catholic, go to Confession as soon as possible, and you're going to feel as free as a breeze. I hope you have gotten courage from Peter, that great man who really and truly loved Jesus.

2

The Armor of God

Ephesians 6:10–19

We are going to look at the sixth chapter of Ephesians, beginning with verse 10, which is on spiritual warfare. St. Paul says to the Ephesians, "Finally, grow strong in the Lord, with the strength of His power."

You know, today this is almost foreign to us, because society tells us that we should grow strong in our own power. We should be positive thinkers, and if we make up our mind to do something, we can do it. Throughout the Gospels, the Epistles, the Acts of the Apostles, and Revelation, we see that a total dependence on God is absolutely necessary for a Christian not only to survive in a world that sometimes seems against it but to grow holy.

I think a lot of people don't even know that they are called to holiness. They think that's for priests and ministers and religious and special people chosen by God to be holy, who kind of wear a halo. By the fact that you are created, you are called to be holy. And Jesus merited for all people—for every man, woman, and child in the whole wide world from now until the end of time and before—to be holy. My guess is we don't understand what it means to be holy.

Living the Scriptures

Is it to pray? Yes! Is it to be good and kind and compassionate? Yes! Is it to overcome our weaknesses and our eccentricities and our failings and our sinful condition? Is that effort? Yes! But what is holiness?

Holiness is to love God so much, that you're willing to depend on Him for your strength. This is something that's ongoing. You can't just grow strong, and all of a sudden, you've got Him. You are not after a diploma. It isn't that you go through a certain amount of theology and a certain amount of everything else, and then you get a diploma. Holiness is for everyone!

Some of our saints couldn't read or write. So where did their holiness come from? Although it's true that the more knowledge you have of God, the more you should thirst for holiness and the more you should acquire it, but that doesn't always follow. Sometimes a peasant can explain to a theologian a problem that the theologian may have pored over for years, because God can work through the uncluttered mind.

We are cluttered. Our minds are cluttered. Our lives are cluttered with everything and anything, and all of it is going to pass. "Very well. Are you saying you shouldn't use whatever God gives you?" No! But a cluttered mind is attached to so many things, where things mean more to it than God. St. Paul is urging us to grow strong in the Lord and with the strength of His power, not our power. He said, "Put God's armor on."

You know, in today's world we don't even understand this one sentence here. He says, "Put God's armour on as to be able to resist the devil's tactics" (v. 11). Why, some of you don't even believe there is a devil! And that, my friends, is the worst thing in the world you can believe, because the verse says "devil's tactics." It doesn't say, "Fight the economy or make war upon this nation or that nation." It says to watch yourself, because your enemy is God's enemy. It's the devil.

You know, there are a lot of ministers and priests who say, "Oh, there is no Hell. God is so compassionate." This has nothing to do with God's compassion. It is because men love evil, and because they love evil, they refuse the good, wondrous, holy God. They create their own Hell. And so, Paul is saying here to put armor on, for it is not human enemies we have to struggle against. But today, all you hear is "human enemies"—this nation and that nation, and we hear of atomic war, and we hear of all the wars that are and could be. There are wars all over the world today. And people are not at peace.

There's war in family life. There are cold wars between husbands and wives. There are all kinds of wars going on. And St. Paul is saying, "I want you to put God's armor on. I want you to use His power and His strength and the salvation that Jesus bought for us—paid dearly to give us." And why? Because he said we are fighting "against the Sovereignties and the Powers who originate the darkness in this world." They are the cause of it. This is "the spiritual army of evil in the heavens" (v. 12).

You know, it's a grave mistake not to know your enemy. Why? Because you don't fight him. You're like a soldier going straight into the battlefield when there are bullets flying all around, because he doesn't see or hear the bullets. And you know what is going to happen to him. It's the same thing in the spiritual war that we constantly have to fight.

And why does St. Paul say "Sovereignties and Powers"? Those are choirs of Angels. There are nine choirs of Angels given to us in Scripture. There are Seraphim, Cherubim, Thrones, Powers, Virtues, Dominions, Principalities, Archangels, and Angels. And St. Paul picks out Sovereignties and Powers. Why? Because when Lucifer fell during the battle in Heaven, he took Angels, which are spirits. He took those spirits from every individual choir, from the highest choir to the lowest choir, and various ones from each one of those choirs—and we call them "choirs" for want of a better word. They are like armies. And so, he says, we are fighting "against the Sovereignties and the Powers."

You are fighting against intellectual beings that are so brilliant, they would make one million Einsteins look pale. I mean, you are in an invisible battle, and some of us go around like there is no tomorrow. St. Paul said that is why you must rely on God's armor, the armor of faith and hope and love and that deep, deep realization—not just knowledge, but realization—that God—the Father, Son, and Holy Spirit—loves you and lives within you, if you are without mortal sin, that is, grievous sin.

So, you have to say, "Why do I have to rely on God's armor?" If you don't, Paul said, "you will not be able to put up any resistance when the worst happens, or have enough resources to hold your ground" (v. 13).

You know what's amazing today? People complain that they don't have time to pray: "I haven't got time to pray. I've got to pick up the kids. I've got to work. When I come home, I'm tired." But you'll find these people watching soap operas. You'll find them going out at night and sometimes carousing all over the place. You will find them with a tremendous amount of time for themselves, but no time for God.

You cannot live in this world and not pray. You cannot live in this world and expect to fight this invisible enemy unless you are a friend of God. Without God, without Jesus, you and I can't do one little bitty thing that's good, let alone fight invisible powers that are much, much greater and much more intelligent than we are.

You know, sometimes I think that one of the reasons we have kind of mentally done away with Hell is because we just don't want any part of a belief that gives us even the remotest idea that there is somebody more intelligent than we are who's evil. Well, a lot of people don't believe in Angels at all. Our pride is so deep sometimes. We don't want to think that there are intelligent beings that are greater and more powerful than we are. And so we kind of skip over these tremendous creations of God.

But my friends, they are your helpers! They are the ones who can help you fight the good fight today. Ask your Angels. You each have a Guardian Angel. The Lord Jesus told us that Himself: "See that you never despise any of these little ones, for I tell you that their angels in heaven are continually in the presence of my Father in heaven" (Matt. 18:10).

Do you think that when you get to be a teenager or an adult, your Guardian Angel just kind of takes off? That's when you *really* need him.

Ask him to help you. Ask him to inspire you. Say, "Angel Guardian dear, give me light. Give me inspiration. Tell me what I'm doing wrong. Give me that grace that I need to know God, to love God, and to serve God."

So, we've got to have that constant reality that we are in need of God. We are in need of intercession in order to fight the good fight. Then, when the world crowds in around you and tells you that all these terrible things are good and right and just, there is something there, a little voice we call conscience that says, "No, this is wrong! It was wrong yesterday. It's wrong today."

And look what he says. Paul says, "So stand your ground, with truth buckled round your waist, and integrity for a breastplate" (v. 14). Think of that for a moment, will you? You know, that's a real meditation: putting on truth, buckled around your waist, and integrity for a breastplate. Paul said, "Wearing for shoes on your feet the eagerness to spread the gospel of peace and always carrying the shield of faith so that you can use it to put out the burning arrows of the evil one" (vv. 15–16).

Well, what does that mean? Has anyone ever tried to lead you into some sin by saying, "Aw, come on. Have another drink. God doesn't care how much you drink." Maybe you've already had four or five. They are inviting you to get drunk, to squander your money, to deprive your family of their needs, of the money that they need to survive.

Gambling is the same. "Oh, go on. You're going to win this time. I mean, blow your whole paycheck." You've got to have enough faith to say, "No. God doesn't want me to do this. It's for my harm. I'm harming myself, my family, and my loved ones."

Your friends come over and say, "Aw, come on. You can take marijuana. You can take crack. You can take all that. I mean, you're strong. You've done it before. You can drink and drive."

You see, you have to have a shield! You have to have something that says, "No!" That's what that shield is. That shield is your will that says no to all these evils that are so strong in the world. But people are so confused; they don't know the truth.

Well then, Paul says, "And then you must accept salvation from God to be your helmet" — he's talking about a war! — "and receive the word of God from the Spirit to use as a sword" (v. 17). So, he takes a soldier, and he looks at him. He sees his helmet. He sees his shield. He sees his bucklers. He sees everything that went on a soldier to protect him in those days, and he turns that around. If many of us had deeper faith, we wouldn't have fallen. If many of us had deeper trust in God, maybe we wouldn't have made some of the mistakes we make. But we have to have courage, and there's always another chance.

Every day is a new sheet of paper on a notepad. Let's pretend that every day on which you mess up is a scribbled mess on a single page. But tomorrow and the day after is a clean sheet, if you are sorry and you repent. Those of you who are Catholic go to the Sacrament of Reconciliation and get rid of these burdens that you carry with you, these spiritual burdens, this guilt, regret, remorse. Make a resolution today that you are going to have a total change of life and root out all these things that bother you. You have short periods of pleasure, but you have long periods of misery.

You know, if we just used common sense, we wouldn't do half the stuff we do—just common sense. I never understand why people who are so sorry at the end of every year for all their sins go out and get drunk the first day of the new year. That doesn't make sense to me.

Well, how are you going to put all this equipment on every morning? Faith and hope and love? Paul tells us how: "Pray all the time" (v. 18). Does that mean I have to have a rosary in my hand or I have to say prayers all the time? Well, you can't. You've got to do your work. You have to clean the house. You have to cook. You may be in an office somewhere. You may have a big position that needs a lot of concentration. But it's that work you do for God. It's the way you do that work. It's the example you give at your workplace—that you refuse to tell dirty jokes or listen to them, that you refuse to lie and to cheat.

I heard of a man recently who quit a very high-paying position. I said, "Why did you quit?" He said, "Because my boss wanted me to do something that was not just or right. It was cheating a customer." He said, "I want to eat, and I want to clothe my kids, and I want to pay rent and gas and electric. But what I don't want to do is lose my soul."

Now, *that* was putting on the breastplate of faith, and that was putting on the armor, because he made a choice. But no one can make that choice unless they pray. You just don't put yourself in temptation and then expect God to come along and save you. People put themselves in occasions of sin, and that's why, if they pray just a little prayer, and it doesn't have to be a long prayer. It doesn't have to be connected with a lot of ceremony. Just say from the depth of your heart, "Jesus, teach me how to act today. Teach me what to say. Tell me what to say. Tell me what to do. Let me do what I do today for Your honor and Your glory. Because You love me so much, I don't want to offend You."

And Paul says, ask Him "for what you need" (v. 18).

"Lord, I don't how to make this decision. I don't know really what's good for my daughter [or my son or my family] at this point. Show me the way. Tell Your Spirit to enlighten me."

Or, "Lord, I don't understand this tragedy in my life. Give me more faith."

Or, "Lord, I feel so disgruntled and so discouraged and so disheartened. Give me hope."

Or, "Lord, I find this person [or that person] at work so hard to love [or my daughter or son or father or mother]. Give me Your love, Lord, that I may love that person."

You've got to do something.

Then Paul says, "Praying in the Spirit on every possible occasion." You know, we have a lot of dead time. We really do. Well, dead time is when you are driving in the car all by yourself, picking up the children, waiting in the doctor's office, going upstairs and downstairs, or walking your dog. To me, that is dead time. Why? Because you are between and betwixt things. Well, you could pray. You can just say, "Lord, I love You," a short, little prayer. In the Catholic Church, we call these ejaculations, aspirations. "Lord, I want to love You like You love Yourself." Just little bitty things. What do they do? They lift your heart and your mind to God. And you can be assured that these tiny, one-sentence prayers, while you're going from one job to another, one office to another, not only are meritorious but they give you the strength to be like Jesus today, to see and discern what's good, what's right, what's wrong, what's bad.

And Paul says, "Never get tired of staying awake to pray for all the saints" (v. 18). I don't know if any of us think we know a saint, let alone praying for all the saints. But who are all the saints? All the Christians. If you are a really good Christian, you are a saint. It isn't somebody in a little niche in a church with a big halo on that makes a saint. It's one who wants to know, love, and serve God in the present moment and is willing to make right choices and sacrifice to accomplish that. It's very simple. And that's why Paul said, "You must stay awake, praying for all the saints."

Do you pray for your fellow Christians? Do you say, "Lord, have mercy on mankind?" Everybody in this world is your brother and sister. Do you intercede before the throne of God for the people in war?

Do we pray for our enemies, whether they are national enemies or personal enemies? Or are we just asking God all the time to give me this and give me that and give me this and give me that?

Then Paul says, "And pray for me to be given an opportunity to open my mouth and speak without fear and give out the mystery of the gospel" (v. 19). Most of us are so afraid of speaking the Name of Jesus, that we haven't gotten this far. So why don't you make a resolution to say every night and every morning, "Lord, increase my faith, hope, and love, that I may be like You, that I may look at my neighbor with the love in the eyes of Jesus, that I may have compassion for an enemy with the compassion of Jesus, that I may forgive as Jesus forgave Peter, that I may be loving as Jesus is loving."

And pray. Prayer is so powerful. It pierces to the very heavens. It attracts the heart and the mind of God when you say, "Father, I praise You! I love You! I want to serve You! I glorify Your Name." Praise Him before you ask for anything. Say, "O God, You are so wonderful. I thank You for all the great things You have done, and I ask You to make me holy as You are holy. Make me compassionate as You are compassionate and loving as You are loving. Bless my children, my friends, my relatives, and bless my enemies, and give this world peace, the kind of peace that can come only from You, Father, and Jesus the Lord."

3

Jesus and the Woman at the Well

John 4:1–34

We are going to look at St. John's Gospel, the fourth chapter. It's an interesting account of something that happened to the Lord; and the reason I'm talking about it is because every one of us, at some time in his or her life, has either done this or at least was sympathetic with the persons involved. So, we want to make Scripture something that is applicable to our daily lives. It can't be something you just read and you say, "Ah, isn't that nice! Isn't that inspiring!" Well, it certainly is nice, and it certainly is inspiring; however, you've got to apply it to your daily life. So I want you to look at this fourth chapter of John and see if you see yourself in it, and then you'll know what to do.

It begins, "When Jesus heard that the Pharisees had found out that He was making and baptising more disciples than John"—well, there's a little bit of jealousy here! — "though in fact it was his disciples who baptised, not Jesus himself" (vv. 1–2).

Jesus never baptized. Isn't that strange? He had His disciples baptize, but it says here Jesus Himself never baptized. Because He is the One Who instituted the Sacrament of Baptism, it was only right that those He had chosen to be the first priests of the New Testament, the first ministers of the New Testament, the first preachers,

21

the first teachers, would be the ones who would begin with that renewal. And yet, the baptism was a baptism of repentance. It was not a baptism in the Spirit until after the redemption.

"Jesus left Judea and went back to Galilee.... On the way he came to the Samaritan town called Sychar, near the land that Jacob gave to his son Joseph" (vv. 3, 5). These are some beautiful little words. Some words in Scripture are so descriptive. I want you to use your imagination again. I want you not only to hear it and read it: I want you to see it happening in your imagination.

"Jacob's well is there and Jesus, tired by the journey, sat straight down by the well" (v. 6). I know I've mentioned this before, but it astounds me that the Son of God, in Whose hands is the whole world, wanted to feel tired just as you and I do. There He is; I mean, He is bushed. And it says, "He sat straight down by the well." Do you know what I mean? Well, just imagine that there is a big well here, and He leaned against the well, and He was just so tired that He — *choo!* — went right down and sat there. The disciples had gone out to look for food. So, Jesus is by Himself at Jacob's well in a Samaritan town.

"It was about the sixth hour. When a Samaritan woman came to draw water ..." (vv. 6–7). Now, this was around noontime, it says, and the women never went to the well at noontime. "Why not?" Well, they didn't. The women went only around six o'clock. And they would gather, and they would gossip. But see, this woman wasn't leading the right kind of life, and she didn't want to be with these other women. And probably, she had tried, and they so humiliated her or spoke very poorly to her that she decided, "I'm going at noon." So, Jesus looked at her. She came to draw water, and he said, "Give me a drink" (v. 7).

She was astounded. And you have to realize the hatred between the Jews and the Samaritans. Samaritans were a kind of a heretical sect. They had designed their own rules, and they built their own temple. They were considered heretics, and you were unclean if you even were seen speaking to one of these Samaritans. Jesus had a real knack for using them, though, especially when He talked about the Good Samaritan, the one who took the man who had been beaten by robbers and put him in the inn and healed his wounds. But this woman was a Samaritan. And so, when the Lord says, "Give me a drink," she is astonished! I mean, what good Jew would ask a Samaritan for a drink when he ran the risk of being unclean? She says, "'What? You are a Jew and you ask me, a Samaritan, for a drink?'—She was astonished. Jews, in fact, do not associate with Samaritans" (v. 9). She is trying to enlighten this Man. "You are probably a stranger in these parts."

Jesus comes out with something so deeply spiritual, which is a great lesson for us. We kind of judge people, and we decide that this person—well, he can't know too much about God, and so we are not going to give him too much, nothing deep anyway. We are going to give him some very basic basics. And after all, this one is a sinner, so what does he know about the Holy Spirit? So, we will give him some basic basics. We make all these kinds of decisions when it comes to teaching someone or drawing back someone who has been away from God.

And Jesus says, "If you only knew what God is offering and who it is that is saying to you: Give me a drink, you would have been the one to ask, and he would have given you living water" (v. 10). Gosh, what an answer! You know, some of us would have said, "Well, as a Jew, what are you doing here? What are you do-ing here at noon? Don't you know that it's not right for women to be here at noontime?" We would have taken up the law, and we would have cut her down to pieces. And the Lord comes up with something deeply spiritual, so spiritual that spiritual writers have been pondering it. And you know, I wonder sometimes if you and I don't say the same thing, or maybe Jesus wouldn't say to us, "If you only knew Who asks you to accept Him. If you only knew the One Who asks you to repent, that you may love Him. If you only knew that One Person, Jesus, Who wants to give you peace and joy. If you only knew the One you are really running like crazy from. If you only knew the love, the intense love that you would find in Jesus. If you only knew you run from the real to the unreal."

I think Jesus could ask this question of all of us: "If you only knew Who it is that seeks you, that hounds you, that keeps after you, that inspires you, that calls you back. *If you only knew.*"

Well, the woman's answer is typical but also astounding. Why? She totally glosses over the profound words He just said. "You have no bucket, sir," she answered, "and the well is deep: how could you get this living water?" (v. 11). She didn't want to hear about anything spiritual. She didn't want to hear Who this Man was. So, she thinks, "This man wants a drink, but He doesn't even have a bucket!"

But you know, the Lord just keeps after her. He doesn't say, "Well, this woman is obviously stupid. She's not getting the point, so I might as well change the point."

Jesus said, "Whoever drinks this water will get thirsty again; but anyone who drinks the water that I shall give will never be thirsty again" (vv. 13–14). Now, what does that mean? That means you will never thirst for the things of this world, for evil, for sin. But once we know Jesus, we will always thirst for Jesus, but it's a living water we get. Why? It's because this living water is something that fills and creates a greater capacity. And so, there is growth, there's depth. And that's a different kind of living water than this woman was talking about; she was interested only in the H_2O that is going to give her something to drink. And yet, a few hours later, she would need more of that.

Jesus was trying to bring her from the purely material to the deeply spiritual. And He says, "The water that I shall give will turn into a spring inside him, welling up to eternal life" (v. 14).

And you know, I think one of the problems with most Christians is that we forget we are to be a deep well. We are to be water that is welling up, just growing and overflowing inside. Jesus is talking about a deeply interior life. This woman was concerned only with exterior things. Well, this woman is humiliated every time she goes to the well. And she is forced to go at noontime, when she's not supposed to go, and that creates a scandal.

So, she says, "Give me some of that water, so that I may never get thirsty and never have to come here again" (v. 15). Always thinking of herself.

Well, now, it's time for Jesus to change the subject. Why? Well, let's see what He asks her. He says, "Go and call your husband ... and come back here" (v. 16).

You see, there was an obstacle to this woman's understanding what He said. There was an obstacle to her receiving this living water. And then He says, "Come back here."

"The woman answered, 'I have no husband'" (v. 17). All of a sudden, I think, she got a prick in her conscience. She said, "I have no husband."

He said, "You are right to say, 'I have no husband'; for although you have had five, the one you have now is not your husband" (vv. 17–18).

You know, some people have a hard time with one of the attributes of God. The one that astounds me and that I relish in is that God acts as though every individual is the only person in the whole wide universe. See, we think we are just a pebble on the beach. We are a grain of sand on the seashore. And so, we consider ourselves in a multitude, and we look down say, "Yeah, God loves everybody." Well, yeah, He loves everybody, but because He is God, because He is inside me and inside you, if we have sanctifying grace, then He knows everything, every thought, every hair that falls from our head as an individual.

Living the Scriptures

And here is another example. When Jesus said to Nathanael, "I saw you under the fig tree," He knew what Nathanael was thinking (John 1:48), and He knows this woman. He knows her thoroughly: "You have had five husbands, and the one you are with now is not your husband."

No wonder they were gossiping about her. Even in the rather permissive society within this world, we still kind of look askance at someone who has had five husbands and is even now living with someone who is not her husband.

"I see you are a prophet, sir,' said the woman (v. 19). She knew it was true, and she admits it's true, in a way. She never says, "I'm sorry." She just says, "Oh, I see you are a prophet."

Now, He hits home too close. You know, we all like religion in some way, but we don't want it to get too close. We don't want it to interfere with our lives. We don't want it to interfere with our consciences. We don't want it to prick our conscience so that we get this feeling—"Uh huh. This isn't good for you." Why is that? Because we want a God Who doesn't "interfere."

But if you're going to spend the rest of your life with Jesus, He has to interfere! He has to provide opportunity. He won't push you. He won't force you. He is so gentle. What a mistake to keep running.

So, the woman does what most of us do when somebody gets too close to our interior life or our private life: she changes the subject, and she gets very religiose.

She says, "Our fathers worshipped on this mountain, while you say Jerusalem is the place where one ought to worship" (v. 20). A change of subject. Some of you have been changing the subject for years. There's going to come a time when you can't change the subject, when you're going to have to face yourself and your conscience and the things you've done wrong and face up to it and say you're sorry and then go on.

26

Well, the Lord is very patient with her. He answers her, "Believe me, woman, the hour is coming when you will worship the Father neither on this mountain nor in Jerusalem. You worship what you do not know; we worship what we do know; for salvation comes from the Jews" (vv. 21–22).

Jesus was telling her something very theological and what was a bone of contention. He said, "Salvation comes from the Jews," which means that, as a Samaritan, she was wrong. "But the hour will come," He says, "in fact, it is here already — when true worshippers will worship the Father in spirit and truth" (v. 23). That's after redemption and Pentecost, when the Kingdom was opened to all men and all women and all children, to all mankind. To the whole world redemption is offered and salvation is offered.

So, what He is telling her is "Don't get hung up on where to worship." He says, "That is the kind of worshipper the Father wants. God is spirit, and those who worship must worship in spirit and truth" (vv. 23–24). "It's my soul, my spirit united with the Spirit of God in truth and holiness and goodness. That's what He wants. Don't worry about mountains and temples. And you must go to church. That is the temple of the Lord, for Catholics especially, where you have the Eucharist."

I called the Eucharist the "lonely sacrament," because Jesus, Who is really and truly present in Body and Blood, Soul and Divinity, is so lonely when very few Catholics today have a deep, deep love for Jesus in the Eucharist. They are so enmeshed in meals and everything else that the Lord's Real Presence is overlooked, and churches sometimes are locked. Sometimes they are closed, sometimes they are not too clean, sometimes very empty. I think that's one of the saddest things in the world today.

Anyway, the woman said, "I know that Messiah — that is, Christ — is coming; and when He comes He will tell us everything"

(v. 25). Not bad for a woman who was such a sinner. At least she knew that much.

And Jesus acknowledges His Messiahship, saying, "I who am speaking to you ... I am he" (v. 26).

Do you know what is so strange about this? Jesus would not answer the Pharisees, the scribes, the Sadducees, or the doctors at the Temple. He asked Peter and the disciples, "Who do men say that I am?" (see Matt. 16:13).

This woman didn't even ask, and she was a sinner, a great sinner, and He just comes out voluntarily and says, "I am He. I am the Messiah. I am the Christ." Isn't it amazing how God has such compassion and love for poor sinners?

At this point, the disciples return, and they were surprised that He was speaking to a woman, a Samaritan at that, but they were too chicken to ask Him about it. Nobody says, "What do you want from her?" or "Why are you talking to her?" (v. 27). They were thinking it. They didn't have the guts to say it.

"The woman put down her water jar" (v. 28). That's another amazing thing about this story. She had come all this way and humiliated herself, and and she puts down her water jar—didn't even get any water—and hurried to the town. She said, "Come and see a man who has told me everything I ever did; I wonder if he is the Christ?" Scripture says: "This brought people out of the town and they started walking toward him" (vv. 29–30).

And then comes a very beautiful sentence. You can see all the people coming. They want to see this Man Who has made such a change in this woman, the town sinner. The apostles get a little edgy, and they, too, want to change the subject. They said, "Rabbi, do have something to eat" (v. 31).

Then comes this marvelous sentence. "I have food to eat that you do not know about.... *My food is to do the will of the one who sent me*" (vv. 32, 34).

I want to leave that with you: "My food is to do the will of the one who sent me." For most of us, unfortunately, the will of God is often not food. It is something that nags us, something we rebel against, something we regret, something that is never quite in union with God's will. But if you want to know what it means to be holy, it is really very simple. This one sentence is all it takes for you and me to become holy. Our food must be to do the will of the One Who sent us into the world. We were chosen by God before time began to be created in this time in history, each one of us with some mission. Maybe we don't even know it. Maybe we will never know it. But whatever we are doing, it is, for this moment anyway, either the permitted or ordained will of God. Make the most of it.

If it's painful, endure it cheerfully. If it's happy, remember from whence comes your happiness. If it's something you regret, put it in the hands of Jesus. If it's something you're sorry about, put it in His mercy. If it's something you fear, put it in His providence. If it's something of the future, trust Him. There is nothing He will not do for you.

So when the Lord says to you, maybe today, maybe tomorrow, "Give me a drink," remember that what He wants from you is your love, your will, and your sins, in that order—your love, your will, and your sins. We have a great God. He is loving. He is compassionate. He gives and gives and never tires, and He is always there. Even when you ignore Him, He never ignores you. Even when you forget Him, He never forgets you. Even when you stray from the right path, He is right behind you, ready to catch you when you fall.

4

Seeing Jesus with the Eyes of Faith

John 4:34–54

I want you to turn to John 4:34. We have already spoken of the Samaritan woman, the woman who went to the well, and Jesus told her everything she had ever done. When the disciples came by, they said, "Rabbi, do have something to eat," to which He said, "I have food to eat that you do not know about. My food is to do the will of the one who sent me."

And really, that's the food for all of us. But we don't always think of the will of God as food. We think of it as a challenge to our own will. You know, here is God's will, and here's my will, and there is this constant turmoil between the two—that's usually what we think about it. And then we think sometimes, "Well, God's will is so adverse to my will."

Well, you see, a lack of faith and humility on our part makes it adverse, because we don't understand that God's will is superior to our will. His will is better than our will and more honest. It's for our good. Sometimes the things we wish for are not for our good. You say, "Well, I don't understand that." Well, at this moment in your living room or den, see if you can look back and say, "Am I glad I didn't get that prayer answered!"

Living the Scriptures

I heard someone say just the other day that he was engaged to someone and now is happy they didn't get married. Well, you see, people are disappointing to us sometimes and people are not what we think they should be. And so are a lot of the prayers that we are just fussing and fuming and crying over, and we almost get bitter against the Lord, but later on, perhaps, we get a little wiser. Who knows? Then it begins to dawn on us. "Thank You, Lord!"

Wouldn't it be nice, though, if we had that attitude *before* it's proven to us that it was the right thing to happen? Well, that's what Jesus is trying to make us all do. He says, "The Father's will is my food." In other words, His human soul was fed by the divinity in Himself and in the Father, and that was the food that carried Him on through the horrible suffering that our redemption cost Him. And so I would like to go over this with you.

If you look at John 4:34, Jesus said, "My food is to do the will of the one who sent me and to complete His work."

What is the work of the Father? The work of the Father is your salvation.

And so, to really want what God wants for you in the present moment—we don't have to like it. It isn't going to be always easy, and it may look very mixed up and confusing at the moment. But we have to have that real assurance that this is because it is permitted or ordained by God, the very best thing; that, at some time in the future, this thing will prove to our good—even when we suffer from evil. Look at the first Christians through the first three hundred years of the Church. They had to hide in catacombs. They were sought out by one emperor after another. They were burned at stakes to give Nero light at night. They were ground up by lions. They were crucified along the wayside. It was terrible!

People say, "Well, what good was that?" The Church flourished. It's amazing how the Church flourishes in times of persecution. The Church seems to go down in times of affluence. Besides that, the people involved were martyrs. They are crowned in Heaven. Those people now are in places so exalted in Heaven, and that's what you and I have to think about. But those of you who perhaps right now are in debt; who are suffering from some terminal disease and in pain; who have the pain of loneliness; those single-parent families and single people who sometimes get so lonely; all of that is like water in a glass, and it's like pouring drop upon drop upon drop. And when you get to the Kingdom, it means more knowledge of God, more beauty, more joy, more happiness. Just phenomenal things happen. So God takes something that's very passing, and then He takes it, and He makes it so beautiful that it's something you would never have dreamed of.

And so that's food: for me to accept the will of God is food. Why is it food? Because I don't feel anxious. I don't feel worried. I don't feel regrets. I don't feel that anxiety that comes in frustration by fighting, fighting, fighting against it. We all know that God wants us to forgive. It's in Scripture everywhere. And Jesus Himself forgave His enemies from the Cross. And yet we don't do it, and yet we know that, if we did, there would be flooding through us peace and joy, kind of like a fifty-pound weight off our backs. By golly, we will hang on to that bitterness. We will hang on to that anger. We just hang on to that unforgiving spirit, as if it was something precious, and it just does us in.

So you see, you are starving on one side, and you are being fed on the other. Doing the will of God and accepting the will of God is food because it feeds your soul. Rebelling against it is starvation. It sucks life and peace right out of you.

Jesus knows what He is talking about. And Jesus said to them, "Have you not got a saying: Four months and then the harvest? Well, I tell you: Look around you, look at the fields; already they are white and ready for harvest! Already the reaper is being paid his wages, already he is bringing in the grain for eternal life, and thus the sower and reaper rejoice together. For here the proverb holds good: one sows; another reaps" (vv. 35–37).

That's what I think about EWTN. We who are here today sow, and you reap. We rejoice together. We sow the seed of programming, the seed of light, of faith and hope. You take it into your heart, you take into your family, into your home, and it begins to grow. The word *broadcast* means "to spread." They used to have bags of seeds, and they would throw it by the handful, and that's what we are doing, and that's what you do every day.

You say, "Well, I don't spread the gospel!" Oh, yes, you do. You spread the gospel by your example, most of all. Your example, most of all, is that one thing that spreads the Good News. It tells people there is a God, and it tells people that God loves them, that God is forgiving and that God is compassionate. Why? Because they see it in you.

Then Jesus says, "I sent you to reap a harvest you had not worked for." What does that mean? "Others worked for it; and you have come into the rewards of their trouble" (v. 38).

Have you realized how long it was, from the time of Adam and Eve, before Jesus came? Prophets and holy men through all those hundreds and hundreds and hundreds and hundreds of years had prayed for a Savior. Prophets came and went — Jeremiah, Isaiah, all the great prophets in the Old Testament, and more, I'm sure, whose words and lives are not written about. All waited. All prayed. All brought the holy people back to God in hopes that He would come among them and deliver them from the tyranny of the world, the enemy, and the flesh.

They had to have a Savior.

When Our Lord was presented in the Temple by Joseph and Mary, who was there? Simeon, an old priest, and Anna, a widow who had been in the Temple day and night, it says, praying for the Messiah to come. These were holy people who could see the corruption in the Church, the corruption in society, and the corruption in the world. And all they could do to say, "Lord, come and save us. Lord, come and deliver us from the tyranny of evil."

They are the ones who sowed. And here the apostles are reaping the fruits of that, because there before them was the very Person these other people worked for and died for, like the Maccabees. Great prophets, such as Elijah, worked, they sowed, they prophesied, and wrote about Him to a *T*, to the very last moment. They described this God-Man Messiah from the moment of His birth to the moment of His death. And here are the apostles, just sitting there, looking at Him — unbelievable.

Well, remember that when He said all this, He was still in that Samaritan town. He stayed there a couple of days. That woman had gone throughout the town and said, "This man has told me everything I ever did." It's remarkable how the people flocked to Jesus. Most people run in the other direction. Most of the people today wouldn't want anybody to be telling them what they did. I think if you are really sincere and love God and want to be with Him in His Kingdom, you want somebody to come out and really tell you.

Well, many Samaritans of that town had believed Him on the strength of the woman's testimony. So, when the Samaritans came up to Him, they begged Him to stay with them. Would you ask someone to stay with you if He could tell you your entire life? You'd say, "Well, I don't think I would like that too well." But what happens if He brought hope with Him, hope and courage and a new life and new strength? Wouldn't that be something wonderful? Well, that isn't something you can look back at and envy the apostles for. You've got it today. You can go to Jesus.

Those of you that are Catholic have the marvelous Sacrament of Reconciliation. You can come home. You can come back. "Though your sins are like scarlet, they shall be as white as snow; though they are red as crimson, they shall be like wool" (Isa. 1:18). The Lord will literally wipe your sins away and never remember them. He will put them behind Him.

And so, you and I have the same opportunity. We don't need to look back and say, "Well, the apostles really had it great. They looked at Jesus face-to-face." Well, it helped most of them, but not all of them. It didn't help Judas. It didn't help the Pharisees. They were still liars and cheaters and murderers. Jesus drew many to God, and many, by the very fact that He was the Son of God, He drew away. Why? Because they loved evil instead of good. And you and I sometimes have to examine ourselves and say, "Well, where do I stand?"

"Where do I stand?" Then He stayed in Sychar for two days. Oh, can you imagine just having Jesus with you for two whole days? He talked to them, and many came to believe.

And they said to the woman, "Now we no longer believe because of what you told us; we have heard Him ourselves and we know that He really is the saviour of the world" (John 4:42).

You know what is strange about that? The Samaritans, who are heretics and are considered unclean by all the good, orthodox Jews in Jerusalem, got the light! They didn't say Jesus was a prophet. They didn't say He was a good man, a holy man. They said He is the Savior of the world. You know, that's why it is so hard for us to criticize other people who we think are kind of off the beam somewhere. Maybe our pride and arrogance and complacency are so engraved, that the Lord doesn't enlighten us. He can't. He can't enlighten us because we don't correspond as this woman did and these people did. Amazing, isn't it?

Well, after these two days, Jesus left for Galilee. Scripture says, "He Himself had declared that there is no respect for a prophet in his own country." He must have been amazed. Here, people didn't have even a third of the grace the Jews had in Jerusalem, didn't have the blessing of God, didn't have any of these things, but they believed. They flocked to Him, and they said He was the Savior of the world. And Jesus was astounded. He said, "A prophet is of no value in his own country."

Then the Gospel says, "He went again to Cana in Galilee, where he had changed the water into wine" (v. 46). Do you remember that? "Now there was a court official there whose son was ill at Capernaum, hearing that Jesus had arrived in Galilee from Judea, he went and asked him to come and cure his son as he was at the point of death" (vv. 46–47).

Do you know what Jesus said? Something very surprising. You are going to be shocked. He said, "So, you will not believe unless you see signs and portents!" (v. 48).

Now, what was wrong with this man's request? Do you remember the centurion, another unbeliever? He said, "Lord, I am not worthy that you should enter under my roof, but only say the word and my servant will be healed" (see Matt. 8:8). He was saying, "You don't have to come and touch my servant. A prophet would have to do that." But you see, this other man really didn't believe Jesus was the Son of God. That's what the Lord is a little teed off about. The man should have said, "Lord, heal my son," not, "Come. Hurry up. He is dying." And that's why the Lord said, "Unless you see signs and wonders, you don't believe. You just don't believe."

"Go home," says Jesus, "your son will live" (v. 50). But Jesus does not go.

What's so amazing is that Jesus, even when He was disappointed in people, gave them miracles. He gave them answers to their problems, even when He was hurt by them. He said, "Nah, go home. Your son is well." He wanted to move this man: "I am the Son of God. I'm not just some prophet."

Scripture continues, "The man believed what Jesus had said and started on his way." You know, some people are so thickheaded.

"And while he was still on the journey back his servants met him with the news that his boy was alive. He asked then when the boy had begun to recover. 'The fever left him yesterday,' they said, 'at the seventh hour.' The father realized that this was exactly the time when Jesus had said, 'Your son will live'" (vv. 50–53).

Jesus didn't perform miracles just to become popular. He always performed a miracle to prove His divinity as the Son of God. And there were two ingredients absolutely necessary: humility and faith. Yet notice this man's faith when the Lord kind of reprimanded him, saying, "So, you will not believe unless you see signs!" Signs are contradictory to faith. Oh, they happen sometimes. But if I see, I don't need to believe. And so, Jesus here wanted to increase this man's faith.

"And he [the man] and all his household believed. This was the second sign given by Jesus, on his return from Judea to Galilee" (vv. 53–54).

You and I, and probably many Christians, were born into Christianity. Many of us worked hard for it. You sought. You struggled. You prayed, and then this great jewel was placed into your hand, this "pearl of great price" (see Matt. 13:45–46). And there is a danger, whether we are converts to Christianity or Catholicity, or whether we've been born into it and just kind of grew up like crops. There's always a danger of taking what we have for granted, not being grateful, taking what the Lord has given us so generously as if we deserved it and not realizing that a large, large percentage of the world does not know Jesus. And of those who do know Jesus, some don't care; they are lukewarm.

And so, when you get it down to the percentage of those people who really love the Lord and are willing to commit their whole lives to Him, or at least live by Christian principles, I bet it boils down to a little group, and I don't mean 10 or 20 percent. You don't have to be a priest or a nun or a minister. Just live by Christian principles. We've got to get ourselves excited again as Christians. If all the Christians in the world were really Christian, the world would be so different, because those who have lost faith would get it back. They would see that Christians have something nobody else has, and that is love and compassion and peace, peace in their hearts no matter what happens.

You see, that's how you preach the gospel. And believe me, that's the best way. On television, I can reach millions of people just sitting there and talking. And you say, "That's a lot of people." No, it's not, because you talk to one person at a time. I don't talk to millions of people: I just talk to you. And then it's up to you to go and multiply that with your family, your friends, your neighbors, and the people you work with.

We could change the world in no time. It's not going to take bombs and political intrigue. It's going to take Jesus and people who love each other. It sounds simplistic, but nothing else has worked—*nothing*. We have been at it politically for centuries. And in every country, there are wars and rumors of wars and hatreds. Newspapers are filled with murders and briberies and suicides.

And so, I don't know about you, but I feel like the prophet Anna, who said, "Lord, come and save us. Come and save us."

So, let us repent, have a change of life and take on the Lord Jesus. And know that you are loved by a great God and that God is loving and merciful and compassionate and that He puts your sins behind Him.

5

Learning from Jesus' Example

Mark 1:35–45

We are going to look at a part of Scripture that many people don't get too excited about. It's the first chapter and thirty-fifth verse from St. Mark's Gospel. Sometimes when we read the Scriptures, we kind of go for the big parables, like the prodigal son and the Samaritan, and we go for the big miracles. And that's okay. But you know, you've got to figure out, you've to reason, before you even talk about faith, why did Jesus come?

You could say, "Many reasons. He came to redeem us. He came to deliver us from Original Sin, to forgive Original Sin, so we would have the capability of entering the Kingdom. He came to make us sons of God. He came to open up Heaven. He came to give us an example of how to suffer in this life and the hidden power of suffering." Well, all of that is true. But I think if we don't look at something else, then you and I are going to miss the boat. And the reason we are going to miss the boat is that we've never known the God-Man, Jesus. We don't know His personality. You and I have to follow Him.

You say, "Well, I follow Him if I keep the commandments."

Yeah, true. But you see, it's not only a matter of following. He has raised you up higher, as the son of God. He has raised you up as friend, no longer a servant. He has raised you up to imitation. Now, how are you going to imitate somebody you don't know and don't know anything about or never met?

And so, the Scriptures allow you to encounter Jesus. You have to encounter God. He can't be a historical figure. Nobody goes around encountering Napoleon or Caesar or anybody else. You must encounter God. We call that a kind of newborn experience, but it happens every day. It should happen every day. I kind of question the "once-in-a-lifetime newborn experience," because every day we need conversion. Every day, we need to know Jesus more and know Him better.

That brings me to my point. How are you going to do that if you don't read the Scriptures and don't try to find out the divine personality of Jesus, so that you, in turn, can change your personality—not your temperament, but your personality—to imitate Jesus? You know, everybody imitates somebody today. The bad part of it is that we don't pick the good people to imitate. We don't have any real heroes or heroines. You see kids going around with these punk hairdos and this clothing that looks like they came from outer space. Why? Because some rock group wears it or some person wears it. A person who's in can change all the styles by wearing a new hat. Well, you see, we are followers!

So, that's what is so important. Whom do you follow? Ask yourself that question: Whom do you follow? I'm going to show you. I want you to look at Mark 1:35. And it's just one of these daily things. It says, "In the morning, long before dawn ..."

You say, "Well, what is so interesting about that?"

Do you ever get up long before dawn? You say, "Wait a minute! I got ten kids. I've got to work. I've been up all night."

I don't think any of us have ever had the schedule Jesus had. He was pushed and shoved and had no time to Himself, but He got up early in the morning. I want to look at the divine personality of Jesus, now. "In the morning, long before dawn, He got up and left the house," probably very quietly, "and went off to a lonely place and prayed there."

He went off to a lonely place and prayed there. Use your imagination a bit. Can you see Jesus now—maybe lying on the floor, a little cushion at His head. And He looks around and sees all the apostles sound asleep. He gets up very quietly and doesn't want to disturb them. He's not one of these people who says, "Well, if I'm up, you're going to be up." He kind of tiptoes out of the house. He looks around. There is hardly anybody else around. He walks slowly, goes up a little hill, perhaps, but there's no one. It's just lonely, probably in the desert someplace where the wind is blowing—sand, little creeks, little animals there, chirping away or whatever animals do at night. Well, He goes off, and He sits on a rock, and He begins to pray.

You say, "Sounds nice." Well, think about it. Don't let it go in one ear and out the other one. I find myself that this time of day is the very best time of day to pray, even if I'm sleepy. Everybody is in bed. Everybody is quiet. There is no traffic, no phones, no bells, just God and you.

Now, I hope something dawned on you. And that is, if Jesus, the Son of God, felt it so necessary to get up before dawn to pray to His Father, what does it mean? He talked to His Father. I wonder what He talked about. Well, He probably talked about the day before, what was coming, the apostles—Judas, perhaps. Maybe He said, "Father, he is going the wrong direction. I've tried very hard, but he won't listen."

I think he prayed somewhere like this and prayed as we do. I think He praised the Father, for His infinite wisdom, which designed such a way for the Messiah to come and redeem us. No one would have thought of it. In fact, it's very hard for most people today—some of them Christian—to believe that.

Living the Scriptures

And yet, He just talked to the Father. But He felt the necessity of talking to the Father. That's what I want to bring out. You know, in today's so-called busy world, we say we don't have time to pray. And we couldn't really get up at four o'clock in the morning to pray, because "I need my sleep." And I don't question that. And I'm not asking you to get up at four o'clock in the morning. But I want you to see something here—all of you who are complaining that you have so much to do.

"Simon and his companions set out in search of him" (v. 36).

They all woke up, and He was gone. He didn't leave a little note like, "See you up on the hill." He was gone. And so, when they found Him, they said—now listen to this: "Everybody is looking for you" (v. 37).

Here, Jesus gets up early so He can be alone and have a little time with the Father, and already, as soon as dawn comes along, the people rush to look for Him. Talk about being busy!

He looked at them and said "Let us go elsewhere, to the neighbouring country towns, so that I can preach there too, because that is why I came."

So, what did Jesus do before He preached? He prayed. And you and I are called by God to be examples of the Word. And example is the greatest way to preach. You may not move your lips, but if your example is good and holy and like Jesus, you have preached a real sermon.

And so, we find here the people are just crowding around Jesus from dawn until it was time to go to bed. There was no time for Himself, hardly time to eat. And there weren't just three, four, or five people. There were crowds of five, ten, fifteen thousand! "And he went all through Galilee, preaching in their synagogues and casting out devils" (v. 39).

See, my friends, we do know how to make excuses. We have a real knack for that. So it seems for me that no matter how busy you are, sometimes examine yourself. How much time do you spend watching soap operas or watching television that really isn't good television or just kind of lying around? You say, "Well, I need to relax." Well, I find prayer very relaxing. You can kick your shoes off and just sit there and talk to the Lord. He is your friend. You don't have to be dignified. He is your friend. So we find that Jesus got up early to pray to prepare Himself to preach the Good News. And whether we preach by words or whether we preach by example, we need to pray. I am convinced that there is such a need for prayer and a need for ceaseless prayer in this day and age.

What do I mean by that? Well, you can't just sit there saying the Rosary all day or saying prayers all day long. Jesus knows you have work to do. You have meals to cook. You have an office to take care of. You have a job. But there are times that I call "dead time." The time that I walk from upstairs to my office downstairs and up again to the monastery. I'm not with anybody. Now, my mind at that time could wonder and worry and think about business and think about this and that. But if I could pull it back and say, "Jesus, I love You. How are You doing today?"

You say, "Oh, come on, Mother, you don't ask God how He is doing today." Why not? I mean, why can't I ask God how He is doing today? I tell Him how I'm doing today. He is a friend! He loves you. You can tell Him anything.

Well, let's go on and see what that day was all about.

"A leper came to him and pleaded on his knees: 'If you want to,' he said, 'you can cure me'" (v. 40).

Now, there is a big difference between this leper and the court official who asked Jesus to come and heal his son who was at the point of death (John 4:47), to whom the Lord said, "So, you will not believe unless you see signs and portents!" This leper knows that Jesus had healed other lepers. And so, he says, "If You want to, You could cure me."

Living the Scriptures

Now, what is so wonderful about that little sentence? It is filled with humility. We are so demanding today, and we make demands of God. I mean, who do you think you are that you can demand of God, as if you are His counselor? You know what the Scriptures say: "Who is His counselor? No one is His counselor" (see Rom. 11:34). But you have to tell Him what He should do. You can ask Him for what you want, but you cannot run around, telling Him what to do!

This leper was humble. He didn't go up to the Lord and say, "I know You can do it. And so I want it, and I want it right now, and I claim it! You must heal me!" He knew that others were cured, but he wasn't. He said, "If You want to." He was willing to wait upon the Lord.

And what does Scripture say? "Feeling sorry for him, Jesus stretched out His hand and touched him. 'Of course, I want to!' he said. 'Be cured'" (v. 41).

Just like that, the leper was healed. Do you see why Jesus had to pray to His Father? Do you see the inner strength He needs as man to do God's work?

"And the leprosy left him at once and he was cured" (v. 42).

I think that kind of healing is fantastic, because the one who wanted to be healed was humble, and he was willing to wait. When you say, "If You want to," that means you are in a position of patience, in a position of waiting. And the Lord felt sorry for him. He said, "Of course, I want to!"

"Jesus immediately sent him away and sternly ordered him ..." You see two different emotions in Jesus. He felt sorry — that's compassion. He was merciful, so He healed him. All of a sudden like that, He stood up and said, "Mind you say nothing to anyone, but go and show yourself to the priest, and make the offering for your healing prescribed by Moses as evidence of your recovery" (vv. 43–44).

You say, "What's going on here?" Well, I don't know. I've seen lepers, and that disease is without question the worst—fingers off, toes off, terrible sores; it's just awful, like being a kind of living dead person. And how could some who was healed of it not be enthused? But Jesus only wanted the man to fulfill the law, which said that if a leper was healed, he had to show himself to the priest so that he could be declared clean and could reenter the synagogue. Jesus wasn't interested in making a big sign and having everybody know it.

Today, you see people advertising, "Come to my healing service." You don't see this in the Gospels. The Lord was not interested in public opinion. "Fulfill the law and go your way in peace." Why was that? Because He knew His time was not yet, and the more He healed, the more of the dead He raised, the more of all the good things He did, the more insanely jealous were the Pharisees and the Sadducees and the priests, the greater their hatred of Him.

And that doesn't even make sense, does it? That doesn't make any more sense than your jealousy or my jealousy or whoever's jealousy. Our jealousies don't ever make sense. They are crazy. We take something away from another person, thinking it is ours. It is not ever ours. It never will be ours. It is a gift from God, whether its beauty or talent or whatever it is. And so, these men who had studied the law, waiting for the Messiah, became jealous just because the Messiah didn't come in the way they thought He was going to come.

That brings up a point. We talk a lot about economic collapse and chastisement and all these things. I'll make a bet, though, it ain't going to come the way we think it is. Even our death won't come in the way we think. You know, sometimes we imagine ourselves dying and make a good meditation, all your people around you, and the priest gives you the Last Sacrament. No, you could go down the street, and somebody hits you head-on. You've had it. So, we can't ever do or say what we think people are going to like.

And so, Jesus didn't want the leper going around, telling the people about this tremendous miracle. The man went away but then started talking about it freely and telling the story everywhere. He did not obey the Lord.

You know, this is phenomenal. You would think if somebody did that much for you, the least you can do is do whatever He asked you to do. And he caused a big problem for Jesus. He caused a big problem, because Scripture says, "So that Jesus could no longer go openly into any town" (v. 45).

Do you know what was amazing to me about Jesus? Even when He did the most wonderful works, He got done in. Do you feel that way sometimes? Do you feel that the more good you do to your neighbor or your husband or wife or children, and the kinder you are, you get done in by the very people you help? That's true of everybody. It's true of Jesus. Now, you see, you are learning something about His personality—very much like your own circumstances, very much like you. Ah, but His response is not like yours and mine. We rebel. We get resentful. We get angry. We get frustrated, agitated at all the others.

Well, He had to stay outside the city in places where nobody lived. Now, wasn't that a terrible thing that man did, in thanksgiving for his leprosy being healed? Well, even so, people went where He was, into the desert.

From Mark 1:35 to 1:45, which is only eleven verses, we learned a lot about Jesus, didn't we? We learned that He prayed a lot and He got up before dawn. We learned that His schedule began at dawn, with people crowding upon Him. We learned that when people came, they asked for cures with a humble heart: "If You you want to." He had great compassion. He said, "Of course, I want to!" We learned He was stern, though, because He knew that if this man ran around telling everybody, He wouldn't be able to go into the city anymore. The man did anyway, and sure enough, Jesus had to run around the desert.

How ungrateful we are to God. We are very ungrateful to the Lord. And sometimes, the more the good Lord does for us, the more we either take it for granted in our pride or we get ungrateful. We don't thank Him. And as a result, He must go away sad.

So don't give God a hard day, a hard time, will you? Let's be a joy to His heart. We must repent of our sins. We know not the time or the hour when He will come. Let's have a metanoia, a whole change of life, a whole change of mind. Let us put on the mind of Jesus, as Jesus had the mind and was the mind of the Father; "He can do only what He sees the Father doing" (John 5:19).

Jesus was so Father-oriented. He was the epitome of the Father. You and I must be imitators of Jesus. We have to. We are victims, sometimes of circumstances, as He was here. But it was all accepted as the Father's holy will. That is holiness. So, try to pray. You don't have to get up at four o'clock in the morning, but there are many times during the day you can pray — in your car, when you're picking up the kids, or on your way to the office.

Let us be Christ-oriented, Jesus-oriented. He loves you. At least say, "Good morning, Lord."

6

Casting Out a Demon

Mark 9:14–29

I would like you to turn to Mark 9:14. When Our Lord would heal, He always looked for a certain ingredient in attitudes—a virtue. In fact, it was so necessary that He wouldn't heal without it. And that was humility. See, we talk about faith, we talk about needing faith to be healed, needing faith in God to pray, needing faith in God even to know He exists. But what is the basis of faith? God gives the grace of faith to everybody. So, why do some have it and some don't?

Well, many times, it's the lack of this special ingredient that we're talking about, and that is humility. You see, if our reason, our intelligence, our intellect cannot see, feel, hear, touch, or understand something in total, then we wipe it off as nonexistent or impossible. It's that simple. So some people will call creation as creating itself. So everything it does is attributed to nature.

Did you ever talk to a tree? Did you ever get an answer from a tree? Did you ever say, "Brother Sun," as St. Francis did, and have the sun speak back to you? No! So, it's absolutely necessary that we understand that the ingredient, the basis, the foundation of faith is humility. I've got to be humble enough to know myself and know the difference between myself and God. I must know that.

Living the Scriptures

I must know that I am very small, finite—that is, limited—and He is unlimited, infinite. I must know I am a sinner and He is all holiness. I must know that there is just so much that I can do and that the amount He does is unlimited and so gigantic—which is to keep the whole universe in His hand, as if it were a grain of sand on the seashore. I have to know that. I have to be awestruck by God. I have to glorify Him and look at His kingdom and say, "Oh, how small I am, and He loves me!"

And so, that's the ingredient; many, many, many times, that's the missing link between God and myself. The missing link is not a gorilla. The missing link is humility, which allows me to see God. So, we're going to find out how Our Lord feels if this is missing, this humility of heart that gives us faith, and what happens when we allow our own limited, finite intellect to stand in front of us and separate us from God.

"They saw a large crowd around them and some scribes arguing with them. The moment they saw Him [Jesus] the whole crowd were struck with amazement and ran to greet him" (vv. 14–15). So, there are some scribes, perhaps Pharisees, explaining the Scriptures to a large crowd of people. All of a sudden, somebody spots Jesus. And maybe they said, "Hey, there's the Master!"

Well, they left the scribes and the Pharisees up there arguing about some little fiddle-faddle. They all turned away and ran to Jesus. I would.

"'What are you arguing about with them?' he asked. A man answered Him from the crowd. 'Master, I have brought my son to you; there is a spirit of dumbness in him, and when it takes hold of him it throws him to the ground and he foams at the mouth and grinds his teeth and goes rigid'" (vv. 16–18).

Well, there's a man who has a son who is not only possessed by a bad spirit, but the bad spirit just throws him on the ground, and he just gets stiff, as when rigor mortis sets in. I'd like you to see if you see yourself in this passage. I see myself sometimes. You know, it's a strange thing. As good as God has been to me and to EWTN, every time the next crisis comes along, we say, "Ah!" Sometimes, just for a moment, we say, "Oh!" But you see, that should never be the case. The God Who took care of yesterday is going to take care of today and tomorrow.

So, let's watch this man and see if we're not a little bit like him. He said, "I asked your disciples to cast it out and they were unable to" (v. 18). Well, you wonder why. I mean, why were the apostles, who had already, as we know, healed the sick, the blind, the deaf, and the lame and delivered people from the influence of the enemy, why is it that this time they couldn't do it? And Jesus gives them a very, very surprising answer. Now, just listen to what the man said: "I asked Your disciples to cast it out and they were unable to." And the Lord said, "You faithless generation. How much longer must I be with you? How much longer must I put up with you? Bring him to me" (v. 19).

Could Our Lord say that to us today? Could He say it to you, to me, and to this modern generation? "You faithless generation, how long am I going to put up with you?" This is not me. This is Jesus.

Now, some of us think the mercy of God is one of these things where you can just presume on His mercy, and that He's going to go on and on, no matter what you do. But this very definitely is indicative of a kind of holy impatience. "How long am I going to put up with you?"

"They brought the boy to him, and as soon as the spirit saw Jesus it threw the boy into convulsions" (v. 20).

You know, you can't imagine that kind of holiness, can you? Most of us would be scared to death of a person who was possessed by an evil spirit—very, very afraid. But you see, our union with the Father is so scattered; it's everywhere. It's here; then it's not here. Then it's here. Then I don't have it; then I have it. It's like pulling the petals off a daisy. "He loves me; he loves me not. I have it; I don't have it. I have it; I don't have it." That's all we are, and you know, sometimes we live our whole lives that way. We find ourselves getting older and older and older, and by golly, we haven't changed a bit. Well, let's see what happens.

"He fell to the ground and lay writhing there, foaming at the mouth." The boy was writhing like a snake all over the ground. "Jesus asked the father, 'How long has this been happening to him?'" Jesus really didn't want to know, of course. He knew. If He knew what was happening to Nathanael under the fig tree, He had to know how long this was going on. But why did He ask? For you and me. "'From childhood' he replied, 'and it has often thrown him into the fire and into the water, in order to destroy him.'" And here is something I bet some of us say every day. I really think it hurts the Lord. Do you hear what he said? "The boy's father said, 'But if you can do anything, have pity on us and help us'" (vv. 20–22).

"But if You can do anything." You see that humility was lacking, and so his faith was lacking. You know, when I see faith today that is made to look like some presumptuous act of pride, I have to question what kind of faith that is, the faith that is so demanding of God. "I want this, Lord, and I want it now! I've done this for You, and You're going to do that for me. And You're going to do it now." I wonder about that, because Jesus always asks for the humility that waited, not knowing what Jesus was going to do but willing to accept whatever it was.

The man said, "Well, Your disciples didn't do it. This boy has been this way since childhood; now if You can do something, do it!" You say, "Well, he didn't have any faith." He didn't have any humility either. You say, "Well, what should he have said?" I think what he should have said is, "Master, if You will, You can heal my son." That would've been deep humility and deep faith. "If You will, You can heal my son." Instead, he said, "Well, look, if You can do anything, do it, will You?"

See how different that is? And when you and I pray, sometimes we pray like that. We say, "Well, Lord, it's a difficult situation. I don't know why I'm even praying for it. Lord, if You can do anything about this situation, please do it. *Please* do it."

And I think the Lord must either laugh at us or get angry sometimes.

"'If you can,' retorted Jesus. 'Everything is possible for anyone who has faith'" (v. 23).

Well, what was this faith? It was to believe that Jesus could do it. See, what Jesus objected to was the word "*Can* you do it?" That's what He objected to. He said, "*Can* You?" He's God! And you're asking God, Who created the boy in the first place, if He can heal him now! If I put something together, I'm the one that can repair it best. So, why do you say, "If You *can?*"

"Immediately the father of the boy cried out, 'I do have faith. Help the little faith I have!'" (v. 24).

Now, we've got the necessary ingredients. He said, "I do have faith. Help the little faith I have." That was that humble act of humility, that total dependence on the Master, that attitude that he was willing to wait. "If I don't have faith, Lord, give it to me. I can't get it by myself. There's no way, Lord. There's no way I can get this by myself. So, Lord, if I don't have it, then give it to me."

Only then does Jesus say, "'Deaf and dumb spirit, I command you: come out of him and never enter him again!' Then throwing the boy into violent convulsions it came out shouting, and the boy lay there so like a corpse that most of them said, 'He is dead.' But Jesus took him by the hand and helped him up, and he was able to stand" (vv. 25–26).

Life puts life back into a body, real life, eternal life, because He says to the enemy, "Never enter him again." He lifts the boy up.

He did that with Peter's mother-in-law; He did that with Jairus's daughter; He did that with the son of the widow of Nain. He reached His hand out and touched him.

Can you imagine what that must have been like? We kind of envy them, huh? We envy the apostles, the disciples and all those who saw this event. But in the mind of God, Who has that marvelous attitude that there's never anything in the past or future, everything is now. As you read this and we go through it, we use our imagination to picture it, and it's happening. It is there, and we're there when it was happening.

Couldn't we say the same, then? Couldn't we say with this man with a heavy sigh, "Lord, I do have faith. Help the little faith I have. Give me grace, Lord. Without You, I am nothing. I can do nothing. And I am worth nothing except what You give to me."

I think the kind of faith that waits upon the Lord is the kind of faith the Lord is looking for today. So far, I think in many areas He would have to say this is a faithless generation. We have faith in men, faith in science, faith in drugs, faith in alcohol. We have faith in sex; we have faith in everything and everyone! People lose their souls in new cults and new religions and new this and new that. "They have itching ears," as the Lord would say (2 Tim. 4:3, RSVCE). They want a God who does exactly as they want Him to do.

Mark 9:28 says, "When He had gone indoors His disciples asked Him privately ..." The apostles didn't have much humility yet. It took some pretty bad falls on Peter's part to get any. Privately — they weren't going to ask Him in front of all these people. They didn't want the people to know why they couldn't deliver the boy.

And so, they said to Him, "Why weren't we able to cast it out?" They began to question. A little pride on their part, because they thought, "Well, if we couldn't do it, He can't do it." It shows you how that little vein of pride runs through everything. You see, if they had faith in Him, as they should have had by this time, they wouldn't have questioned, "Why weren't we able to do it?" They should have known that without Him they couldn't do anything! They had no power on their own to heal the sick and the dying and all the rest.

" 'This is the kind,' Jesus answered, 'that can only be driven out by prayer' " (v. 29).

Now, some books say "prayer and fasting," but "fasting" is not in the original text. Some scribe must have put that in. It's okay, though. But let's just take it the way it is here, that this kind is delivered, driven out, He said, only by prayer. What did He mean?

I'll tell you what He meant. The apostles were frightened — frightened at the boy's terrible condition, frightened at the crowd — and they began to think of themselves. And when they did that, their power just went out of them. Why? Because they were no longer using the power of Jesus, no longer using the power He gave them. They were beginning to take this power into themselves.

And what did He mean by prayer? When we pray, we are united to the Holy One — the Lord Jesus, the Lord Father, the Lord Spirit. We are united to the Trinity. And if the apostles had prayed, had they forgotten the crowd, had they forgot even the terrible condition of this young man and depended entirely on the power of Jesus, the Lord, the power of the Father, that infinite, holy, omnipotent power for Whom nothing is impossible — *nothing* — if they had depended on that, if they had united their tiny little gifts and strengths to that power, they would have healed that boy and delivered him.

You know, it's a great lesson, the lesson you and I must hear and heed. Because it's a lesson that will help us to become holy as He wants us to become holy. He wants you to become a saint. Call upon His mercy. It's like the ocean. It's vast and has no depth and no limits. Though your sin be as wide and long as the world, it is not beyond His mercy. So, before you retire tonight, go to Jesus with a humble heart and say, "Jesus, I am poor in spirit. I have nothing unless You give it to me. Lord, increase my faith, increase my hope, increase my love."

7

A Meal at a Pharisee's House

Luke 7:36–50

We're going to look at St. Luke's Gospel. And we're going to take something I think that all of us need. We've heard it, like almost everything in Scripture, at least ten times — in church or maybe your own reading. But anyway, I want you to turn to Luke 7:36, and we're going to take it all the way down to verse 50, because I think it's something that you and I need to know. It says, "One of Pharisees invited Him to a meal." Now, you have to know that the Pharisees were not in any way friends of Jesus. They did not approve. They were jealous of Him. He intimidated them. But anyway, one of them invites Jesus to dinner.

You and I, knowing this, would probably not have gone to this dinner. We would have said, "Well, I'm too busy." In other words, if we know we've been invited by an enemy to go and have dinner, we'd probably say, "Hey, I know you. You're just going to insult me. So, why should I bother?" So we probably would not have gone.

But Jesus went. That's the difference, you see, between Jesus and the rest of us. "When He arrived at the Pharisee's house and took His place at the table, a woman came in, who had a bad name in the town." Now, there's a lot of controversy over this. Who is this woman? Some say it was not Mary Magdalene; some say it was not

59

the sister of Martha, and they go on and on and on and on. But I feel it was. Now, you don't have to take my word for it, but we do know that Mary of Magdala was a sinner. And I would think the probability of this being her is very good. "She had heard he was dining with the Pharisee and had brought with her an alabaster jar of ointment" (vv. 36–37).

Now, you have to know that men in those days, when they had these banquets, ate alone. The women were not invited. In fact, a woman would not have entered the house of this particular Pharisee. You have to wonder why the servants let her in, unless she had been there before on business. And so, "she waited behind Jesus at his feet" (v. 38). And you have to realize that, in those days, they reclined at the table, you know, kind of very comfortable like. They had these divans that were big and wide, and they lay on their left sides, and they ate with their right hands. They kind of dipped everything in one bowl.

And she brings this jar of ointment, an alabaster jar. Now, an alabaster jar is a marble jar that would have been extremely expensive. She waited and she knelt at the feet of Jesus, "weeping, and her tears fell on his feet" (v. 38).

I think sometimes those of you who perhaps have had great sins in your life, or still have them, would understand what it must have meant for her to kneel at the feet of Jesus, what relief must have been there. It is no question that He had seen her before and forgave her all her sins. She was a woman who was of ill repute, commonly known as a prostitute. Probably lost her dignity—obviously, she did—her self-respect. She had no respect from anyone else. She was, as it says in Scripture, "a sinner." And as such, I think she felt at the very bottom of the barrel. She had degraded her body, her soul, her spirit, her mind, her heart. She was a little garbage heap.

And suddenly, the mercy and the forgiveness and the love of Jesus had reached out at some point and looked at her with the kind of love that only Jesus could give or the kind of gaze that only Jesus could give and said, "Your sins are forgiven."

You know, Catholics are often criticized for having a sacrament of Confession. And the reason we're criticized is because, "Oh, you go to confess to a man." Listen, I've heard some pretty heavy confessions on television lately. I mean, not only to a man, but to the whole world. I don't think we can criticize Catholics for Confession anymore. But there's no one there on television who really says to you, as Jesus had probably said to this woman—which she heard with her ears—"Your sins are forgiven."

You need to hear that. You need to hear it. It's that cleansing process. Your neighbor can forgive you, but it's important that God forgives you. So, when I hear people saying, "My priest says there's no need for Confession," I shiver. I shiver! Oh, I don't know how anybody could say that, unless he's deaf, dumb, and blind! You need to confess your sins and get them forgiven! You need to hear from Jesus, "I forgive you." You have to be healed from all those tendencies that keep pushing you in those occasions of sin.

You get the idea today that some people think we're immaculately conceived. We're a bunch of spoiled kids on this earth, where we can just get as dirty and filthy as we want to get, and God says, "Ah, you look really cute that way." Horrible! Sin is horrible. It crucified Jesus. Well, sometimes I think when I keep saying this, I'm hitting a brick wall. I hope not. If you're like Mary Magdalene or anybody else, it doesn't matter what kind of sins you've committed. Sin is sin. It offends God and offends man. It ruins your soul. Get cleaned up. There's no reason to stay that way. Just read this passage and kind of feel what the sinner must have felt as she knelt at the feet of Jesus: "she covered his feet with kisses" (v. 38). She had sinned much. She was repentant.

Let me tell you something about repentance. Most people think that repentance is only saying, "I'm sorry." Whenever I say, "I'm sorry," I have got to repair for that damage. How do I repair to God? Right here, this is how you repair. He took upon Himself your sins and my sins, and this is what happened to Him. But real repentance is not regret. Some people think if they regret they've sinned, they are repentant. No, that just says, "I'm sorry I did it." There's no concept there of whom I offended, whom I hurt, whom I destroyed. It's just, "I did it. I can't believe I did it."

That's regret! But repentance — I think the perfect repentance would be if I looked at God and said, "Lord God, I have sinned against You. I have sinned against heaven and earth. I'm sorry. I thank You for Your infinite mercy that first shows me my sin and makes me feel sorry and then envelops me in the ocean of mercy and envelops me in love, wraps me in love as if I were a wounded bird. And then You carry me in Your hand. Thank You, Lord. I love You."

I think that if we could do that, we would be repentant, and this is exactly what this woman did. "She waited behind him at his feet, weeping, and her tears fell on his feet, and she wiped them away with her hair." Long hair, maybe to her waist, probably a very beautiful woman. She takes that long hair and pulls it around and begins to wipe His feet. "And she covered his feet with kisses and anointed them with the ointment" (v. 38).

Now, the Pharisee, who was a hypocrite and a liar and a cheat and a proud man, was in darkness. He had no regrets, no repentance. He was a perfect man in his own eyes. "He said to himself" — notice he didn't say it out loud — " 'If this man were a prophet, He would know who this woman is that is touching Him and what a bad name she has.' " I wonder how he knew. "Then Jesus took him up and said, 'Simon, I have something to say to you.' 'Speak, Master,' was the reply. 'There was once a creditor who had two men in his debt; one owed him five hundred denarii, the other fifty. They were unable to pay, so he pardoned them both. Which of them will love him more?' " (vv. 39–42).

A Meal at a Pharisee's House

I mean, five hundred denarii and fifty. Now, which one do you
think loved him more? Well, the Pharisee's getting a little bit edgy.
His own conscience is beginning to bother him. "'The one who
was pardoned more, I suppose,' answered Simon." He knows what's
coming. He's no dummy. "Jesus said, 'You are right.'" The one who
was forgiven more probably loved more.

"Then He turned to the woman," the one everybody was looking
down on, the one everyone was looking at with a kind of horror.
"'Simon,' he said, 'you see this woman?'" (vv. 43–44). Now, everybody had seen this woman! There are only men at the table. There
are only men there, and probably a great group of men, because
the apostles were there, the Pharisee had other friends, and there
were other Pharisees, and some of them wanted to see this Jesus
firsthand. They had quite a gathering—all men.

But Jesus says, "Do you see this woman?" But He wasn't saying,
"Do you see her with your physical eyes?" He was asking, "Do you
know this woman?"

To the Pharisee, He says, "I came into your house." Do you
remember in the beginning we said Jesus knew this man was out to
get Him? That's why he invited Him to dinner. You and I wouldn't
have gone to that dinner. We would have just stayed home. "And
you poured no water over my feet." What did that mean? In the
East, hospitality is a godly virtue. It's very important in the East,
extremely important! It's a scandal not to be hospitable. And so, the
guests had their feet washed by the host. And you have to admit,
they walked in the sand. They had left their sandals go at the door,
and the host knelt and washed the feet of every guest who came in.

And they skipped Jesus. He washed everybody's feet except
Jesus'—the Lord of all, the One Who created him. He did not
wash His feet. Jesus was there to be insulted. And that was the first
insult! And the Lord said, "You did not wash my feet." What a hurt
that must have been for Jesus. "But she has poured out her tears

over my feet and wiped them away with her hair. You gave me no kiss" (vv. 44–45). Another insult. When you came in the house as a guest, the host went up to you and kissed you. But when Jesus came in the door, the Pharisee looked at Him and turned around and kissed someone else. And Jesus felt that. All of you who sin and say, "Well, God doesn't care. He doesn't feel it." He felt that!

And He says, "'You did not anoint my head with oil, but she has anointed my feet with ointment." Well, it was quite a ceremony when you went to dinner. "'And I tell you,' he said to the Pharisee, 'For this reason I tell you that her sins, her many sins, must have been forgiven her, or she would not have shown such great love. It is the man who is forgiven little who shows little love.' And then he said to her, 'Your sins are forgiven'" (vv. 46–48).

Now, right away they started. It all went over their heads. Every bit of light, every bit of grace that Jesus was trying to give these people went *psst!* Because now their first uncritical thought was, "Who is this man, that he even forgives sins?" That shows where they were. "But Jesus said to the woman, 'Your faith has saved you; go in peace'" (vv. 49–50).

Jesus was not concerned with what people say. When people think adversely about us, we change our attitude so we're accepted by them. And Jesus was not that kind of God-Man. You took Him as He was, or you left Him.

You know, I hope this is a consolation for so many of you reading this, even you youngsters and teenagers. You've gotten yourself in a web. You've gotten yourself in the wrong crowd, and you don't have the guts to get away. But believe me, make the break. Shed your tears of grateful repentance, loving repentance. Don't just be sorry because you did it or you ruined your dignity or you ruined your life. That's enough, but it isn't enough. Do what this woman did: cover His feet with your tears. And if you can't cry, and some can't, those of you who are Catholic have that wondrous Sacrament of Confession, and I hope you don't attend a parish that doesn't have Confession or has it for a half hour for two thousand families.

Find yourself a priest who will listen to you and can say to you, as Jesus said to this woman, "Your sins are forgiven." There is no greater gift in the world. There's no greater gift than to know that God and I are friends again. We're not enemies, we're friends again. Everybody makes mistakes. Don't live in your past. Take this moment that Jesus is offering to you with this book. And though your sins be as great and high as Mount Everest, go to Him. Go to Confession, if you're Catholic. Listen to the words "I absolve you of all your sins."

And the Lord says something very important! "Your faith has saved you; go in peace." It takes faith to confess your sins; it takes faith to see God in a man. These Pharisees did not have it. They did not. It takes faith to say, "Lord God, forgive me. Forgive me." We must be sorry; we must ask forgiveness; we must make reparation. And we have such a loving, compassionate God, that if we're sincere, the ocean of His mercy covers us and wraps us in His love. To those who have sinned much, I say to you: "Love much." And we're all great sinners in one form or another. We're like St. Paul. We don't do the things we want to do, and we do the things we don't want to do (see Rom. 7:15). We're always in that state of a *seesaw*.

But let's go up on that seesaw. Let's give ourselves to Jesus. I ask the Lord to call you to repentance, to call you to reparation, to call you to love much, to call you to give the overflow of that love to your neighbor. He, too, needs to hear from you, "I forgive You." They are the sweetest words man has ever spoken outside of "I love you."

8

Putting God First

Luke 13:31–15

We're going to look at what I call "scriptural tidbits." It's not the particular event or story or parable the Lord was going to tell us. It's just a lot of little things that happened that kind of manifest the divine personality of Jesus. This is the God-Man sent by the Father Whom you and I are to imitate. If you want to know how to be a Christian, this is it. You see Jesus. You see how He acted under every possible circumstance. And when those circumstances come into our lives — not the same but at least similar — then we know at least how we should act. But if we don't, we can always be humble and repentant and repair, which we call reparation.

So I'd like you to turn to St. Luke's Gospel, to the thirteenth chapter. And one of these little tidbits I'd like you to look at is verse 31. I want to bring this out, because I feel there's a tremendous amount of misdirected compassion in the world today. Now you say, "What is that?" Well, we can have compassion. We should have compassion. In fact, Jesus said, "Be compassionate as your Father is compassionate" (Luke 6:36).

And we're not that way. We have misdirected compassion many, many, many times. And that means, for example, if someone is living a life of sin and they are very close to us, we won't say anything, because we don't want to hurt their feelings, we don't want to spoil their friendship, or we don't want to make them feel guilty. So, we don't say anything. And we give them the impression that what they're doing is right and okay. And that's misdirected compassion.

We don't have to condemn, and you shouldn't condemn. And we cannot judge, but we have to look at it. The Lord said, "You will be able to tell them by their fruits" (Matt. 7:16). And if you know they're doing something very bad and they're going in the wrong direction, then at least you can say, "Hey, I love you, and I hate to see you keep doing this, because you're going to lose your soul."

And it doesn't have to be Hell and brimstone. We have to call a spade a spade, but you don't have to do it in a harsh way. And you say, "Well, I don't like to make people feel guilty." You have to make them feel guilty with the *right kind* of guilt. Not the guilt that is wrong or bad or resentful or bitter or despairing—that's not the right kind of guilt. But a sensitivity to God, a sensitivity to sin.

We very, very seldom hear about sin in sermons anymore, very seldom, nonexistent because we want everybody to be happy! Well, I'm more concerned, and you should be more concerned, about your eternal happiness than this temporary happiness. And nobody says it doesn't take a lot of guts or a lot of sacrifice, but the Kingdom is worth it. We're talking about an eternity of Heaven or an eternity of never-ending Hell.

And so let's look at Jesus. And here at the time it says, "Just at this time some Pharisees came up. 'Go away,' they said. 'Leave this place, because Herod means to kill you'" (v. 31). Well, how would you like it if somebody came up to you and said, "Hey, you'd better get out of here. Somebody's going to kill you."

Do you know what Jesus said? He said, "You may go and give that fox this message." *That fox.* I wouldn't want to be called a fox by Jesus. He called the man what he was. He didn't go around and say, "Well, you know, why don't you explain to Herod that I mean well and that, you know, I wish him no harm?" Jesus didn't come off with this sugarcoated kind of answer. He said, "You may go and give that fox this message: Learn that today and tomorrow I cast out devils and on the third day attain my end" (v. 32).

What was He telling him? That Herod was not the one to decide when He would go, when He would die. And He said, "For today and tomorrow and the next day I must go on, since it would not be right for a prophet to die outside Jerusalem" (v. 33).

And we learn that the Lord called a spade a spade, and He put Herod and those Pharisees in their place. Why? Because Jesus saw the Father in every single thing that happened to Him. He knew they were out to kill Him. And when He raised Lazarus from the dead, that was the last straw for all of them, including Judas. Suddenly, Judas realized this man was not going to be a political leader. He was not going to deliver Israel from the hands of Caesar. There was not going to be money in his pocket. Judas thought the same way as we do in so many things today: "What's in it for me? And if there's not anything in it for me, then you're expendable."

Executives sometimes get to the high positions they're in by walking over anybody and everybody—they are expendable—because they want a position, they want a salary, they want popularity; whatever it is they want, whatever ambition drives them. I think Our Lord could say that to quite a few of us, "You fox." We always look at the gentle, compassionate Jesus, but that didn't keep Him from telling the truth. He had a great emphasis in His voice. He wouldn't say mildly, "Go tell that little fox." He'd say sternly, "Go tell that fox." He knew what He was talking about.

And then He said something that was so sad. He said, "Jerusalem, Jerusalem, you that kill the prophets and stone those who are sent to you! How often have I longed to gather your children, as a hen gathers her brood under her wings, and you refused!" (v. 34). Do you know what He's saying? Do we kill the prophets and stone those sent to us? I think we do it today quite a bit. Oh, we don't do it with real stones, but we do it with verbal stones. We don't really kill them, but we manage to slaughter their reputations, their credibility. We bemoan the work they do. Sometimes people will lie and cheat and slander just to destroy another person. Isn't that killing the one who is witnessing to Jesus?

Or when we throw verbal rocks at the Holy Father, because he is so strong and brave enough to tell you what God wants you to hear? I have heard him stoned verbally many a time in newspapers, magazines, commentary news, and conventions. We're no different. How many times is there some real Christian witness in a community, and somebody suddenly begins to start, "Oh, I knew them when ..." When what? So we dig up as much dirt as possible to destroy a new beginning, a new birth. Oh, we do a lot of that today!

And the Lord looked at all this very sadly, and then He told how He wished it had been. Did you ever have a wish list? They're nice. But they don't always happen. It's nice sometimes to have a wish list. He said, "How often ..." This was Jesus' wish list. "How often have I longed to gather you"—longed, really wanted to so badly. To do what? "To gather your children"—He's talking to Jerusalem now—"as a hen gathers her brood under her wings" (v. 34).

Did you ever see a hen do that? Oh, you city folks missed something, because it's wonderful to see. We have chickens. And last year we had a few little chickies. It was wonderful to see those little chicks just run. If there was any danger, if there was anything at all, they just ran under the hen's wings, and you never knew they were around. They were very quiet, and they just stood there, nice and comfortable. And this is so important, and that's why Jesus used that as a picture, because we don't understand words. We have to see pictures!

And so He said, "That's what I wanted to do with you! I wanted to gather you under my wing, to protect you, to guard you, so that you wouldn't have to do all these things. You wouldn't have to suffer all this. But you would not. I gave you Ten Commandments that said, 'This is how you treat your body, because I made it.'" And He would say, "And I told you that, because then you'd live the happiest life, the best life, the cleanest life, the purest life, the life of God, because you're made in His image, but you would not. I wanted you to be holy. I sacrificed my life to give you everything you have, to give you salvation, to give you Heaven, eternal happiness, eternal joy, and you would not. I have done everything I could to the last drop of my blood and you would not."

Well, you know what He said after that? "So be it." That's what it says here. "If that's what you want, okay. So be it."

You know, that kind of sends the shivers up my spine. But since you refuse, the Lord says, "So be it." The Lord just says, "Okay. If that's what you want, that's what you can have." And then He says, "Your house will be left to you. Yes, I promise you, you shall not see me till the time comes when you say, 'Blessings on him who comes in the name of the Lord'" (v. 35).

So, we have a tremendous lesson in this. I call them "little tidbits." I call them the *hidden* sufferings of Jesus. We don't always think about them. And we think—especially during Lent—about the Agony in the Garden and the arrest and the terrible trial and carrying the Cross, the Crucifixion. And it's very pictorial in our minds. But the hidden sufferings of Jesus, the night He was in the dungeon, in prison overnight, waiting for dawn—the lack of understanding He had among His own apostles, the inability of them to understand the simplest parable. To work three years and then have people say, "Lord, what did You mean?" To know that He was going to die and leave them, and they still didn't understand, and these were the men He picked to found a new Church! I mean, talk about suffering: He had it.

I guess one of the worst was right here. There are two things here. The first is what He suffered in the Agony in the Garden, and that was to see so many souls like these who refused His grace, His love, His salvation—to know that even though He would suffer and die and rise for each one of us as if no one else existed, so many would choose to be lost. You choose. God doesn't send you to Hell. They chose. He said, "So be it. You don't want to be with me in my Kingdom. You don't want eternal happiness. You want the tinsel of this world. You want the momentary pleasures of this world. You want to blow your mind on drugs and soak it in alcohol, so you don't even know where you're going. You want to take the image of myself in you and obliterate it."

He won't stop you. He will hound you. He will give you grace upon grace to change, but if you refuse to the very bitter end, you put yourself in Gehenna.

And there is something else here—the longing of Jesus to love you, to forgive you, to protect you. "I long," He says, "to gather you as a hen gathers her brood, and you would not."

There's a beautiful picture. I don't remember who it was that painted it. It shows Our Lord sitting on this rock, and you see the Temple in the distance in Jerusalem, and He's sitting over there, and He's very sad, and there are tears coming down His eyes. And it said, I think, underneath, "If you only knew who it is that calls to you, that beckons you to come."

You and I sometimes kind of get angry with Adam and Eve, and we say, "Well, if it wasn't for you, we wouldn't have all this pain and suffering and starvation and injustice and tragedy and all." But I don't know. We don't do too hot with all the graces, and having Jesus in our midst, and then the Church having the Eucharist and Mary, that immaculate, wondrous woman. We push all these gifts aside, and we get so smart. We decide that we know how it all came altogether. We have a lot of little gods walking around, but there is only one God. There is only one sovereign Lord, and that is the Father, the Creator of all things; the Son, the Redeemer of all; and the Spirit, the Sanctifier. Without Them, there is nothing.

And you and I want to be among those who say often, "Jesus, Savior, I need You. Put me under Your wing. Protect me from the flesh, the world, and the enemy. Give me the grace to know You and to love You and to serve You and acknowledge You as sovereign Lord of all things. I may not understand the stars and the moon, and I may not be able to explain light-years or black holes or galaxies and quasars. I may not be able to understand how they split an atom. It really doesn't matter, as long as I know the God of all atoms, the God who created every single one out of nothing—*nothing*."

Physicists and scientists and doctors explain what already is, or they think they explain, except centuries later somebody else comes along and just blows their theory out of the box. You cannot fathom the wisdom of God. You can explain an eye to me and tell me how it works and operate on it and change it, but you cannot create.

I have a brace on; it's kind of a bulky thing. It takes all of that to do what a single little nerve can do. A man at his best is bulky, noisy, Godless is the silence.

I saw a twig while looking out the window this morning. It looked like an ordinary twig on a tree, a little branch. It looked as if it was dead. And suddenly I looked again, and you know what? It had tiny, tiny little leaves that broke through what looked like a dead branch and in total silence. I never heard a sound.

So, I think all of us need to kind of get our priorities together. Put God as number one. Give Him your love, your time, your heart, your mind, your soul, your strength. All these newfangled cults and all the rest of them give you nothing, because they are not the Creator of all. They are man-made idols to tickle ears and push you in the wrong direction. So be careful of those who say, "He is there," and "He is there," and "He is here," for no one knows the time or the hour when He comes. And one day, He will come for you and me. Make your choice now. Make your choice to want to be with Him, and make the sacrifice it may take to do that, whatever it is.

He thought you were worth this. Tell Him you think He's worth whatever it is you need to give up.

9

Jesus Feeds the Five Thousand
and Walks on Water

Mark 6:29–52

In our Scripture, we're going to look at St. Mark's Gospel. St. Mark is, I think next to John, my favorite Gospel, because he puts in a lot of details that the other Evangelists don't put in — for example, when they were out at sea and Our Lord was sleeping in the boat and St. Mark said, "His Head was on a cushion" (4:38). It's one of those nice, little additions that kind of give you a better picture. And so, in His account of the feeding of the crowd, the multitude, he said there was tall grass there. So, there again, you get a real picture of a great crowd and yet tall grass. So, I like St. Mark, because he seems to add these little human touches.

So, if you look at St. Mark's Gospel, we have here a kind of sad account of where St. John the Baptist was beheaded. Many of the apostles and disciples of Jesus were at one time disciples of John the Baptist. And so, it said, "When John's disciples heard about this, they came and took his body and laid it in a tomb." So, the apostles had rejoined Jesus and told Him not only about that but all the other things that they did and all the things they taught. And He said to them, "You must come away to some lonely place all by yourselves and rest for a while" (vv. 29–31).

75

Now, that's an amazing sentence, because in today's whirlwind age, when everybody is go, go, go, go, go, we hardly ever think of going to a lonely place and resting a while. Even our vacations are rushed. Most people come home a couple of days earlier just to read after a vacation. I always thought a vacation was something where you would rest, but it doesn't always turn out that way. So the Lord said, "It's time, now. You've been working very hard, and we're going to go." And He said, "For there were so many coming and going that the apostles had no time to eat" (v. 31).

Now, I want you to remember that little sentence. There were so many people around Jesus all the time, that they had to kind of control the crowd and protect Jesus and get people to Him at the right time. And ah! It must have been horrendous. And so, they were tired. "So they went off in a boat to a lonely place where they could be by themselves" (v. 32).

You know, that's really nice. Wouldn't it be nice if families did that, instead of fussing and fuming at each other all the time? It would be wonderful if, as it says here, "they went off in a boat to a lonely place where they could be by themselves"—especially all your families struggling and fighting all the time and arguing and fussing and fuming. Maybe you're too noisy. Maybe you need to find some lonely place in the woods, some little old cabin somewhere, and just go there for a weekend and say, "Hey, why don't we find a different atmosphere, without noise, in God's nature and just talk this thing over, get our priorities together, get our wits together, forgive each other, and start over?" So, that's apparently what the Lord wanted to do. I would imagine these apostles would get a little bit edgy.

"But people saw them going, and many could guess where; and from every town they all hurried to the place on foot and reached it before them" (v. 33). Can you imagine yourself trying to get away from a huge crowd of people and thinking you got this all figured out, and you go to some place, and before you get there, they are already there? I can just see those apostles. Their nerves are frazzled! They are hungry. You know a lot more than I do that men get grouchy when they're hungry. They've worked hard, and they are hungry, and they're trying to get away from the crowd. And they're looking forward to a nice, peaceful meal together, and the people are there again.

"So as he stepped ashore he saw a large crowd; he took pity on them because they were like sheep without a shepherd, and he set himself to teach them at some length" (v. 34).

You know, Jesus is so absolutely, totally selfless. I know some of us may have just said, "Wait a minute, everybody, give me a chance to eat, and I'll be back." Or we would've turned the boat around and went in the other direction. You know, Jesus took pity on them. He forgot that He was also hungry, and He was also tired. He forgot all that. The pity He had for the crowd was greater than His own hunger and His own fatigue. Talk about knowing what to do. He's teaching us in every way—by His words, by His example, by how He reacts. So, He talked to them at some length. Now, He didn't say, "Look, I'm going to give you a five-minute lesson. It's getting late, so you should all go home." No. "It was getting very late, and his disciples came up to him" (v. 35).

I mean, they're counting the minutes by this time. And "Hey, this is a lonely place, and it's getting very late, send them away so they can go to the farms and villages and buy themselves something to eat" (see v. 36). Like going to McDonald's or Burger King or whatever. "Go to the restaurant and buy yourself something to eat; it's getting late." But the Lord said the most phenomenal thing. He said, "Give them something to eat yourselves" (v. 37).

And they were astounded. Now, keep in mind that these are frazzled apostles—hungry. It's getting late. They're impatient with Jesus. They're angry at the crowd that they found them out and had the nerve to get there before them and, worse yet, wouldn't permit them to eat. And Jesus says, "No, you feed them." I mean, can you imagine feeding and serving them! It's not just preparing something, but it's serving five thousand people! Five thousand people is a lot of people! That was five thousand men—they didn't even count women and children in those days. Well, the apostles are getting a little edgy, and they said, "Are we to go and spend two hundred denarii on bread for them to eat?" (v. 37).

In other words, they were impatient with the Lord. They said, "Hey, look. We've got two hundred denarii." It wasn't bad, two hundred denarii, "But are we going to spend all of this and buy some food?" In other words, "What are you talking about?"

"'How many loaves have you?' he asked. 'Go and see.' And when they had found out they said, 'Five loaves and two fish.' Then he ordered them to get all the people together in groups on the green grass, and they sat down on the ground in squares of hundreds and fifties" (vv. 38–40). Now, I just want you to know and to understand what the Lord was doing and the demand He made among these apostles. They're already hungry, already tired, already impatient. And He said, "I want you to feed these people, and I want you to put them in squares, this way and square them off in fifties and hundreds." Now, you got one hundred people sitting in a square and fifty people sitting in a square. So, the Lord demanded that they sit them down, count them, and put them in squares. He said, "Hey, get them in fifties and let them sit down." He made more demands on them.

You know what happens to you and me. I mean, we already got twenty-five hundred other problems and troubles and anxieties and then—*poof!*—another one, another one, another one, another one, another one.

That's exactly what He did here. "Then he took the five loaves and the two fish, raised his eyes to Heaven and said the blessing;

then he broke the loaves and handed them to his disciples to distribute among the people" (v. 41). See, Jesus did that. He kept breaking these two loaves, breaking and breaking and it never, never went down. And He just kept filling their baskets, and then there were the two fish. "They all ate as much as they wanted" (v. 42).

Can you imagine that? Now, five thousand people, not including women and children, may have been ten thousand people. Some people eat a lot! And it said, "They ate all they wanted." Well, I'm sure they didn't. I would imagine that fish was something like in the Italian districts in Philadelphia and New York, where they have what my Grandma used to call *baccala*. It was dried codfish. It would be hung up in the stores, and you went and bought one, and then you soaked it in water, and it all came back up and you boiled it. And she used to make fantastic soup with that, very inexpensive.

"They collected twelve basketfuls of scraps of bread and pieces of fish" (v. 43). In St. Luke's Gospel, and St. John's, it says that when they collected it, they had seven baskets; that was the second time. This time, it's twelve basketfuls. Well, that's another thing the Lord demanded. I'm supposing the apostles ate as they served someone else. There was tall grass there, we know that from St. Mark, but the Lord demanded they pick up the scraps.

I would have said, "Okay, everybody, take the tall grass, bury your scraps," because you know, you're taking scraps from everybody, and they were all strangers to the apostles. If you had a big party and you had five thousand people, you know how people are at a party or a big doing. You know, when I'm at a banquet, I leave two-thirds of my plate, because it's just always too much food, and who wants to eat at eight o'clock at night and then give a talk? So, there's just a lot of food that's left over.

And Jesus said to them, "Pick it up." Now, the apostles are frazzled, nervous, angry, hungry, and have had crowds around them all day long, and the Lord says, "Put them into squares, feed them, now pick it up." You think you're pushed? "Pick it up."

You have to wonder what happened to those twelve baskets, you know. I bet those apostles ate out of them for six months. It was dried fish. Nobody's going to carry around fresh fish in the desert all day long, at least no one you would get very close to you. "Those who had eaten the loaves numbered five thousand men" (v. 44).

I'll bet the feminists want it to say five thousand *persons*, but it would be wrong. It was five thousand men. Well, now, are you under the impression that Jesus is finished with these apostles? I mean, don't you think He has pushed their virtue level to the nth degree? Well, He's not finished with them. He has some common pity on them: "Directly after this he made his disciples get into the boat and go on ahead to Bethsaida, while he himself sent the crowd away" (v. 45). Jesus said, "You go on. I'm going to send the crowd away. I'm going take all these people, and I'm going to say goodbye." See, Jesus was never, never tired of reaching the people. He just wasn't. He fed them. It would have been sufficient to feed these people, bless them, and go with the apostles, and no one would have ever found faults—*no one!* But you know what? Jesus went that extra mile again.

You and I have limits to our love, to our compassion, to our hospitality. We definitely have limits. And you say, "Hey, I'm tired. I've had a hard day. Give me a break." And Jesus never said, "Give me a break." He said, "I'll send the crowd away. You go."

"And after saying good-bye to them"—to the crowds, maybe blessing a little child and patting somebody on the head and healing somebody—"he went off into the hills to pray" (v. 46). And that's another thing about Jesus. He could have said, "Hey, I am dead tired. I'm just going to lie here and go to bed, and I'm going to go to sleep under the stars. You apostles go your way; the crowd will go home; I'm going to stay here. Nobody bother me, please."

No. He had done His work. He had done it well. He had to talk to His Father. Isn't it strange that you and I always say we're too busy, that we don't have enough time, enough is enough, I've got to do this, I've got to do that? Jesus, the Son of God, found it necessary in His human nature to pray.

Well, He's not through with those apostles yet. "When evening came, the boat was far out on the lake, and he was alone on the land. He could see that they were worn out with rowing, for the wind was against them" (vv. 47–48). So, there they were rowing. They've had a hard day. Now they're having a hard night. "And about the fourth watch" — He made them wait practically the whole night — "he came toward them, walking on the lake." And they were petrified. They saw Him coming, and you know what's so wonderful about this incident? "He was going to pass them by" (v. 48).

He had pushed their virtue level to the very nth degree. And when they saw Him coming, instead of coming into the boat, He started going in another direction. Why? He wanted them to call out in the midst of their problems, anxieties, frustrations. He wanted to hear them say, "Lord, help us!"

Exactly what He wants to hear you say. And so often, we get bitter, we get angry with God, because He's not going to get into your boat or my boat unless we invite Him. He is a gentleman.

Scripture says they were terrified. And at once He said to them, "Courage! It is I! Do not be afraid" (v. 50). When you think you've been pushed to a point when you can't take it anymore, you cry out to Him and He's going to say the same thing to you. "Courage! It is I! Do not be afraid."

"Then he got into the boat with them, and the wind dropped immediately. They were utterly and completely dumbfounded" (v. 51). I would say *dumbfounded* is kind of hardly a descriptive word. They were, I don't know, astonished. They were numb, kind of frightened, because "they had not seen what the miracle of the loaves meant; their minds were closed" (v. 52).

And you wonder, "Where did this sentence come from, and what does it have to do with this?" The miracle of the loaves proved His divinity. Only God can make something out of nothing or multiply something little into a great amount of bread and fish. But they didn't understand that. They missed the entire message. And because they missed the message of the symbol of the Eucharist—the feeding of the five thousand with the loaves and the fish, when they all got the fish, all got the loaves—so it is with the Eucharist. You all get Jesus, the whole Jesus. And because their minds were closed to that, their minds were closed to the miracle of His walking on the water. That should not have dumbfounded them. It should not have terrified them. Their minds were closed, and they were closed because they were so agitated that they could not see God.

They were upset. They were disgruntled. They were tired. They were unhappy with Jesus. They were unhappy with the crowd. And now, they had wind. Their whole souls were just in a state of agitation. So they missed the miracle of the loaves and the fish because their own souls, concentrated and self-centered, were so alive to themselves, they missed the miracle. And so, the only thing they could be is terrified, and they never kept their eyes on Jesus. And that's why His answer was, "Courage! It is I! Do not be afraid."

You see, when we allow a thing or the present moment or the conditions of the present moment to so possess us that we cannot cry out to God in our helplessness and ask Him to come to our aid and save us. Your mind will remain closed until you can say, "Lord God, I am a sinner. I have sinned against Thee. I am sorry. Forgive me. Pour Your ocean of mercy over me. Pour Your Precious Blood over me. Give me the courage and the strength I need to withstand this cross, this temptation, this incident, this person, this place, that I may always hear Your voice, that I may see, that my mind will not be closed to Your presence around me." And that's what Our Lord was saying: "It is I." Their minds were closed to the presence of God in the midst of the storm. And you and I do the same thing over and over and over.

So, my friends, we ask the Lord today or tonight to give us an open mind, that no matter what happens, no matter how distraught or agitated or fearful we are, we can look up as the apostles did during another incident and see no one but Jesus.

10

Jesus Heals a Demoniac

Mark 4:39–41 and 5:1–20

We are going to look at the fourth and fifth chapters of the Gospel of St. Mark. Jesus had just quieted the storm. The apostles were out at sea, and Jesus was asleep in the stern of the boat. And St. Mark has those little extra details: he said Christ's head was on a cushion, tired, sleepy. Well, it looked as if they were going to drown, water coming in, the storm twirling the boat around, and Jesus just sound asleep. So finally, right before chapter 5, Peter, in his fear and terror of the storm—and you and I would think he had every right to be terror-stricken—said, "Master, do you not care? We are going down!" (4:39).

And then there must've been just a kind of silence, not from the storm, but from their very fear. Jesus woke up and first looked at the storm. He said, "'Quiet now! Be calm!' And the wind dropped, and all was calm again. Then he said to them, 'Why are you so frightened? How is it that you have no faith?'" (vv. 39–40).

Well, when you look at that, you say, "Lord, we're drowning. The boat is literally sinking." I don't think Our Lord was angry but more disappointed here, because they were afraid of the storm. It says they were almost swamped. I think it's when Peter says, "Master, do You not care? We are going down!"—I think that's what hurt

Jesus. I really do. He knew. Because isn't it strange He woke up, and He said, "Be calm"? He talked to the storm first. And you and I are in the storms of our life, in the tragedies we don't understand, in the illness that is so long, in the conversions that we pray and pray and pray for, and nothing seems to happen—I think we all do that, don't you? We cry out, "Master! Don't You hear me? Don't You care?" I think that's what hurts Him most. He knows. He cares.

And you wonder what should have been their attitude? What should have been the apostles' attitude? I think the attitude should've been, since they've seen so many miracles, that nothing could have happened to them. They would not have gone down. They may have had to fight the storm till they hit shore. They would not have gone down, because Jesus was in their boat.

And you and I can say the same thing. It may appear they were going down. It may appear we're getting lost in that way. But if we know Jesus and we love Jesus and we're trying to please Jesus, we're never going to be lost. He will always be there.

So, it was in this kind of frame of mind that "they reached the country of the Gerasenes on the other side of the lake, and no sooner had He left the boat than a man with an unclean spirit [he was possessed] came from the tombs toward Him. The man lived in the tombs and no one could secure him anymore, even with a chain" (5:1–3). This was a man who obviously was mentally deranged, a demoniac, a man who was possessed by an evil spirit. "He had often been secured with fetters and chains but had snapped the chains and broken the fetters, and no one had the strength to control him. All night and all day, among the tombs and in the mountains, he would howl and gash himself with stones" (vv. 4–5).

That whole city must've been absolutely terrified. You know, sometimes you read in the paper that somebody is robbing every particular house in the city, in an area, in a neighborhood, and the people are petrified. And it just puts fear into them. They didn't know what he was going to do. And to wake up in the middle of the night and hear somebody howling in the tombs …

"Catching sight of Jesus from a distance, he ran up and fell at His feet and shouted at the top of his voice, 'What do you want from me, Jesus, Son of the Most High God? Swear by God you will not torture me!'" You know why he said that? Ordinarily, a possessed person would run away from Jesus. Well, it says, "For Jesus had been saying to him"—as soon as Jesus got out of the boat, He saw this demoniac in the distance, and immediately Jesus started to say—"come out of the man, unclean spirit" (vv. 6–8). And the man, without any control, was drawn to Jesus. And the evil spirit in this man was saying, "Don't torment us. What do you want with us?" It was not really the man who spoke.

"What is your name?" Jesus asked. But Jesus wasn't talking to the man. Jesus was talking to the evil spirit within that man.

"'My name is legion,' he answered, 'for there are many of us.'" Oh, imagine that. There wasn't just one demon in this poor man; there were many demons in this poor man.

"And he begged him earnestly not to send them out of the district. Now there was on the mountainside a great herd of pigs feeding" (vv. 9–11). A great herd of pigs. Now, you know that pigs were unclean in the Jewish ritual of those days. And if you ate any pork, you were unclean. You could not go to the Temple. "And the unclean spirits begged him, 'Send us to the pigs, let us go into them'" (v. 12). They didn't want to go down where they belonged.

So, He said, "Go." The power of Jesus! Now, listen to this. With that one provision, "Get out," they came out of the man. "Go," and they went.

Scripture says, "With that, the unclean spirits came out and went into the pigs, and the herd of about two thousand pigs …" I don't know if you've ever had a pig. Years ago, we raised a pig, and it was something. I cannot imagine the odor from two thousand pigs! But the enemies, the demons said, "We are legion" in this poor man. What this poor man had done to permit himself to be so possessed, I don't know. But two thousand pigs "charged down the cliff into the lake, and there they were drowned" (v. 13).

You can just about imagine those herdsmen. One minute, they've got two thousand pigs, and all of a sudden, they don't have any pigs. And maybe ten of those pigs belonged to this person and twenty to that person, maybe one hundred or one thousand to another farmer, and all of a sudden, they were gone! And you know, this brings up something I think is extremely important. The Lord would rather have you lose everything than to lose your soul. This man was lost and was made whole again at the cost of two thousand pigs.

You say, "You mean salvation costs?" Yes, sometimes it costs you stopping a sinful life. It costs you giving up the pleasure — that's what some people call it, a pleasure — getting drunk at night, taking drugs. There are a lot of things man calls pleasure that are very sinful and separate a person from God. Yeah, it is better that you lose it or you lose the ability or the opportunity. It's better for these pigs to get lost than for you to get lost. Remember that. I think everybody has some pigs in their possession, meaning the sinful things that keep us away from Jesus, keep us away from salvation, and keep us away from being the loving, kind, compassionate, empathetic people Jesus wants us to be., The loving people that Jesus wants us to be.

So, you know this was not a very popular thing for Jesus to do, because the swine herdsmen ran off. They didn't want to be responsible for two thousand pigs. And they said, "That demoniac is healed! Some prophet came off a boat and sent all the demons into your pigs!" They didn't know Jesus yet. Many of them didn't believe in Him yet. Well, the people were horror-stricken. And that's something very interesting. It says here, "And the people came to see what had really happened. They came to Jesus and saw the demoniac sitting there, clothed and in his full senses—the very man who had had the legion in him before—and they were afraid" (vv. 14–5).

The people were afraid. They saw God at work, and they saw God before them, and they were afraid. You know, that happens today a lot. God can deliver you. He can be so good to you. He can do so many things, and the more miracles we see, the more afraid we get. Instead of saying, "O God, You are so wonderful! How great Thou art," instead of going up to Jesus and saying, "Oh, thank You. This man was a menace to our community. We lived in fear during the day and in terror during the night. Thank You. So, it cost me a few pigs. Thank You. You must be the Messiah, for no one has helped this man before!" Wouldn't you think that's what they should have said? Well, they didn't. "And those who had witnessed it reported what had happened to the demoniac and what had become of the pigs" (v. 16).

And this is, I think, one of the saddest passages in Scripture: "Then they"—the people of the town who had lost their pigs— "began to implore Jesus to leave the neighborhood" (v. 17). Can you imagine that! "They began to implore Jesus to leave the neighborhood." You know, that's unbelievable. I mean, Jesus should have been carried around the city like a hero. It isn't like they lost their living or that they lost everything they had. I suppose everybody in the village had a couple of pigs, but they shouldn't have had any, because they were Jews. And even if they were not Jews, part of owning pigs was their living and part was for their food, but that doesn't mean they were cleaned out. So, you have to ask yourself a question: "Where were their priorities?"

They would prefer the Lord Messiah Jesus, the Eternal Word, leave the district, because they lost some pigs. And many say, "Well, that is kind of terrible." But I wonder, though, if we don't do that sometimes, if we don't say, "Jesus, You're welcome into my home, as long as You do what I want You to do. Jesus, You're my friend, as long as You obey me, as long as You give me everything I pray for and everything I ask. Jesus, I will believe in You, as long as I'm healthy, I'm wealthy, and I'm wise. But don't let suffering or pain or disillusionment or dissatisfaction or disappointment come my way—if You let those touch me, then, Lord, leave this neighborhood. I want the good life."

Isn't that the same? Isn't that the same as these people did? We don't want Him on a cross. We want Him this way, nice and clean. We don't want a reminder of how painful love is. This is too much of a witness. We don't want a painful love. We want a love that's all pleasure and joy and happiness.

Well, if you do, then you don't love like Him, because this is how He loves. And these people had everything that was good, given to them free by this great, good Jesus. You know what it means to implore somebody? It means to say, "Will you *please* leave this place?"

Can you imagine asking Jesus to leave your home? Well, I think we all do that sometimes in many ways. "God didn't answer my prayer, so what's the use of going to church?" Somebody told me not too long ago that all the hypocrites go to church. I said, "Well, they can stand one more. Go ahead. You go, too."

You know, it's amazing what we do to God still. With all our knowledge, we have made such technical advances, scientific advances, and electronic advances. Spiritually, we are not even in the Middle Ages. You say, "Oh, come now, Mother, I see a lot of good things going on around the world today."

Well, then why isn't the world better? Why isn't there peace in families, in cities, in nations, in the world? We can't hide our head under a bushel forever.

Well, they implored Him to leave. And so, He got into the boat. Jesus is such a gentleman. He will not stay where He is not wanted.

Jesus Heals a Demoniac

"As He was getting into the boat, the man who had been possessed begged to be allowed to stay with him" (v. 18). You can just see the man saying, "Lord, let me go with You!" He must have felt terribly uncomfortable. These people didn't want this man, well or sick. They sure enough didn't want him as a demoniac, but they had nothing they could do with it. They were afraid of him. He was stronger than they were. But they didn't even want him well, because it was a constant reminder of what happened and of the power of Jesus!

So, Jesus says something that I think is very strange. I would've taken the man with me. But Jesus was so loving toward the people who preferred pigs to Him that He said to the man, "Go home to your people and tell them all that the Lord in his mercy has done for you" (v. 19). He called Himself Lord. "Tell them all that the Lord in His mercy has done for you"—the *Lord* in His mercy.

You see, it's such a sad thing, isn't it, that we have an opportunity of spreading the gospel? We, too, have an opportunity of telling everybody what the Lord has done—the mercy He has bestowed upon us. You could say, "Oh, well, Mother, I'm not a great sinner. I've been good all my life." Well, I've got news for you, that goodness, and the things you have done and the commandments you have kept, is a special gift of grace from the Lord God. And no question, you responded, and you said yes. There is that beautiful cooperation between God and the soul. They must say yes together. That's what holiness is all about. I think that we need to examine our consciences a little bit.

"So the man went off and proceeded to spread throughout the Decapolis all that Jesus had done for him. And everyone was amazed" (v. 20). This man had fantastic witness power, because there was the man who was mad and possessed by legions of demons, and there he was walking around perfectly normal. "Everyone was amazed."

Living the Scriptures

And that's another thing about our Christianity in the Gospel. We are amazed at Jesus! We are amazed at what He did in this book! We are amazed at the power God! But it never affects our life enough to change us. Now, that doesn't seem to make any sense to me, that you can be so convinced of His love, His power and then do nothing about it. See? So, I am sad to say and you're sad hear that things haven't changed that much.

But we must change them, you and I. Conversion and transformation begin here in your own heart, in your own mind. From there, it works into your family, from your family to your neighborhood. It has to build from the family unit. And until we get our families together, until we get our nation together, until we go back to Jesus, until we are repentant, asking for forgiveness, until we bow our heads and say as a country, as a nation, as a world, as a people, "Lord, forgive us, we have sinned against Thee in Heaven," only then will we have peace.

He loves you very much.

11

Jesus and the Syrophoenician Woman

Mark 7:24–25 and Matthew 15:21–28

We are going to look at two Gospels—St. Mark and St. Matthew. First, we will look at St. Mark's Gospel—Mark 7:24. And this is about the Syrophoenician woman who begs Jesus for a cure. And this is very important, because I think it has happened in everybody's life at some time or another. We don't understand, and as a result, we sometimes can be tempted to be bitter against God, lose our faith sometimes, or just get very lukewarm—all of which are just bad fruit of something intended by God to be something very good. When you look at Mark 7:24, you find this.

"[Jesus] left that place and set out for the territory of Tyre. There He went into a house and did not want anyone to know He was there but He could not pass unrecognized" (Mark 7:24). He probably thought, "Well, we will just have a nice evening together," and He was looking forward maybe to supper. He had already had a hard day working with crowds and people and curing and healing and delivering, and His human nature was perhaps getting a little tired. Well, as they are walking down the road, "a woman whose little daughter had an unclean spirit heard about Him *straightaway* and came and fell at His feet" (Mark 7:25).

Now, we are talking about someone small. How little is little? Well, it could be anywhere from four years old to eleven or twelve. Her "little daughter had an unclean spirit." We are really not too sure what that means. Could someone little, young, be possessed by a demon? Could it have been an illness that they attributed to evil but was just an ordinary physical ailment? Whatever it means, she heard that Jesus was in the vicinity.

St. Mark uses the word "straightaway" a lot. When St. John talks about the woman at the well, he says, "He went straightaway"; He just straightaway went *boom*, sat near the well, so tired. So, in Mark the word "straightaway" means the woman rushed. She ran to find Jesus. And we have to know that a very, very important aspect of our spiritual life is to run for Jesus. We don't have to be perfect. You know, you're not going to some kind of debutante party where you meet some famous man or a famous celebrity that you get all dressed up for. This woman was in need. She was probably just hysterical. She didn't care how she looked. She didn't wait until she had her finest dress on and looked her best. When somebody said, "Jesus is here," she ran straightaway. And you and I should do that. We should be extremely careful that we don't fall into a Jansenistic heresy, which meant you had to be very, very pure and very, very clean, and very, very everything. You had to be almost sinless to even speak to God. That's a terrible thing.

So she just ran the way she was. And you need to run to God just the way you are, with all your sins, with all your weaknesses, with all your guilt, with all your frustrations. You can't wait until they suddenly calm down, because He is the only One Who can calm them down. You can't wait until they are gone. He is the only Who that can get rid of them. You can't wait until you feel good about them. He is the only One Who can make you feel good. You just can't wait for that opportune time and place. And so many people do that. They wait and say, "Well, I've got to have a good time now. When I get old …"

In other words, you dedicate your later years to Him. You don't even know if you're going to reach a later year. You don't have time to do that. You have got to run to Jesus now, straightaway. Now is the time—today. This is the moment. This book may be your moment of healing, of conversion, of transformation, of a change of life. Now is the time. Go to Him right now, straightaway. That's what this woman did, and she came and fell at His feet.

Let's turn to Matthew 15:22, because it has a little more detail than Mark does. It says that before she went and fell at His feet, she "started shouting, 'Sir, Son of David, take pity on me! My daughter is tormented by a devil.'" What a heart-rending plea! And Jesus is so compassionate, so loving. Well, He never answered her a word. He didn't say a word. He kept on walking as if He never heard her. Isn't that a turnaround? And His disciples—now, this is unusual too—they were shocked! They must've looked at Jesus and said, "What in the world is happening?"

"His disciples went and pleaded with Him. 'Give her what she wants,' they said, 'because she is shouting after us'" (Matt. 15:23). Now, their motivation was not good at all. They had absolutely no sympathy for this woman. They weren't sorry because her daughter was obviously, as it says here in St. Matthew, "tormented by a demon." Again, it may have been some illness, but this is the word he used. They said, "Give her what she wants because she is shouting after us." They wanted to get rid of the inconvenience of having this woman follow them and shout after them. I feel so sorry for this woman, because Jesus is not paying any attention to her, and the apostles think she is one big pain in the neck. No sympathy, no compassion from anyone.

Well, Jesus finally says something. And I bet the apostles were thinking, "Oh, now He is going to heal her, and we will be at peace." But you know what He said? "I was sent only to the lost sheep of the House of Israel" (Matt. 15:24). This means if He is going to heal anybody, it's going to be a Jew, not a pagan. Well, the apostles had never heard this before. I'm sure they agreed, but they never saw Jesus in this kind of frame of mind.

The woman, though, is undaunted. She comes up now, and she kneels at His feet. She stops Him along the road. He can't move, now. She is smack in front of Him on the ground. She says, "Lord." I want you to read this, now. In the beginning, she says, "Sir, Son of David, take pity on me." First it was "sir." Now she says, "Lord." What a woman is this! I mean, she had been rebuked by Jesus, by His silence. She had been insulted by the apostles, telling her literally, "Will you close your mouth? Keep your mouth shut. You're pestering us." And she goes from "sir" to "Lord."

When Jesus said, "I was sent only to the lost sheep of the House of Israel," I think most of us would have just said, "Okay, if that's how You feel about it." We probably would have turned around and gone away, disgruntled, bitter, and resentful because He hadn't answered our prayer. He did not answer our plea. We would have said He lacks compassion. We would have gone through a whole list of terrible things, and we would have missed a miracle. This is a marvelous instance. To me, it's one that is so filled with our poor human nature and the hidden wisdom of God that is so far above our reason and our wisdom, that we cannot comprehend.

And so she said, "Lord, help me" (Matt. 15:25). Well, she goes from "sir" to "Lord," and she kneels at His feet, and she is pleading. Now, I'm sure, if you were a disciple there, you would have said, "Ah, what a woman. I feel sorry for her. The Lord is certainly going to give her what she wants."

Not so. Boy, does He say something here. He says, "It is not fair to take the children's food and throw it to the house-dogs" (Matt. 5:26). That means pets. It's just not fair. "It's not fair that I take the food from the children of Israel, for this is where I was sent." He said that before: I was sent to heal Israel. So, it's not fair to take the food, the power that is theirs at this point, and give it to a house dog, a pet.

Well, had you and I persevered this far, I am pretty sure that 99 percent of us would have gotten up at this point and just cried and run away as fast as possible. But you know what she says? Something unbelievable. She says, "Ah yes, sir." She agrees with Him. She says, "Ah yes, sir. But even house-dogs can eat the scraps that fall from their master's table" (Matt. 15:27).

She is absolutely phenomenal, and she is a pagan! She doesn't know the true God. Jesus is astounded—astounded! And I bet the apostles just stood there with their mouths wide open. Why? You know, we are a strange breed, because we just don't understand. We just don't understand God. And Jesus said to her, "Woman, you have great faith. Let your wish be granted" (Matt. 5:28).

Well, we have to ask some questions. In the first place, it was true. The Messiah came from the Jews, and as such, Jesus came to save them, to culminate, to finish, to end the Old Testament and begin the New. And this woman was sorely tried. She was rebuked. She was refused, but she just keeps on. And here we find a woman so humble. And you know what's so strange is the humility of these pagans. The centurion, for example, who said to Jesus, "Sir, I am not worthy to have you under my roof. For I am under authority myself, and have soldiers under me; and I say to one man: Go, and he goes; to another: Come here, and he comes.... Just give the word and my servant will be cured" (see Matt. 8:8–9).

What humility! We see humility in the prostitute, the great sinner in the house of the Pharisee, who went in and wept over the feet of Jesus and wiped those feet with her hair. We find that humility, that necessary ingredient, finally, in the woman at the well. She says, "Come and see a man who told me everything I ever did." Humility. And these were people who didn't know God.

Living the Scriptures

This woman with the tormented daughter has some tremendous lessons for you and me. The first lesson is humility. She said, "Ah yes, you're right. I am a house-dog. But even house-dogs eat the crumbs." You know, Jesus could never have at that point done anything but give her what she wants. Why? Because she was so humble. She persevered. Oh, if you want to talk about perseverance, this is a marvelous lesson in perseverance.

And you and I wonder sometimes, "Why did Jesus do this?" And why does Jesus make us wait and wait and wait, and we plead, and we beg. He knew this woman. He knew what was in her. And He brought out a depth of faith that astounded His apostles and is a consolation to all of us throughout the centuries. Persevering prayer under the most adverse circumstances, under those conditions where you think God has forgotten or God has just kind of pushed us aside or God is not answering our prayer or God is saying no. In all those circumstances, we have to know that if He is delaying an answer to what we think we need—I say that, because sometimes we really don't know what we need—we can be assured that He is bringing out of us the very best in us, not the worst. He is bringing out of us those things that have been hidden for years, that depth of faith and hope and love and adherence to His will over our will. And in the spiritual life, those are so important! Those are the things that make you holy. Those are the things that make you great before God—not what you possess, not your riches, not your talents, not your gifts.

What this woman did and how the Lord literally drew out of her a depth of faith we would have never thought possible: that's what's important in life, not these temporary joys and these temporary things that we grasp for and hang on to as if there were nothing else. And while we are hanging on, they are slipping out of our hand and our grasp. It's like trying to go up a greased pole. You get so far, and while you're getting there, you are already sliding down. Well, it's important, I think, that you and I understand.

And I wanted to bring out, along with this, something on the next page of Matthew. In Matthew 16:24, it says, "If anyone wants to be a follower of mine, let him renounce himself and take up his cross and follow me." That's exactly what that woman did. Oh, she was asking for her daughter to be healed, but she had never laid down her cross. And her cross right then and there was not only her daughter's health, but a refusal from the Lord. It looked like He was just going to ignore her, but His heart must have been quickened. And what does He say here? He says, "For anyone who wants to save his life will lose it" (Matt. 16:25). This woman wasn't worried about herself. She wasn't worried about the humiliation. She wasn't worried about the insult. She didn't think of herself at all. She was totally selfless. She had no human respect for the apostles, saying, "What are these men going to think of me? I'm pestering them!" Jesus said, "But anyone who loses his life for my sake will find it" (Matt. 16:25). She was willing to lose her life, and that's what you do when you have persevering prayer.

There are things that are conditional in life. In other words, I'm not going to get them unless I ask for them. And for some of them, I need to ask and ask and ask, and some things I'm going to get whether I ask or not. I never asked for a TV studio. I would have gotten it whether I asked or not. Things evolved, and it came to be. So there are some missions and things like that that you're going to get without asking, but most things in our life are conditional.

Why does God allow that? The Lord was building up in that Syrophoenician woman a great hope and a great faith. And when it got built up to a certain degree, He said, "Yes." Because He is not going to treat us like spoiled children and just give us everything we want. He wants to build up those things that are most important—our faith, our hope, and our love. And that's a cross to carry. It's a cross that we have to keep on plodding ahead when we don't feel like it, when we have to pray when we feel dry as bones, when we have to continue being good under very trying circumstances. It's difficult. But God is building your faith and your hope. And He is saying to you, "Continue. I am up here, ready to help. I'm going to give it to you, but you must be ready to accept what I want to give. You must have the capacity to withhold what I want to give you. And so I must try you. I must test you. I must make you wait at this point. But don't stop."

Keep on praying. Keep on persevering. Because sometimes even when I don't get the very thing I'm asking for, I always get more faith, more hope, and more love. And these are the three virtues that expand my capacity to know God, to love God, and to see God in a clearer way, to understand Him better in the Kingdom, where it's forever and ever and ever and ever and never, never, never, never ending. We cannot imagine something that will never end! But everything we touch, everything we see, everything we are—people come, they are born, they die—has an end. But the soul has no end!

It is in the soul that Jesus is mostly interested in us—He takes care of us, body and soul. His providence is in every facet of our lives from morning until evening. So put your trust in Jesus. He loves you. He cares for you. He may seem not to answer, but His love is always there.

12

Without Perception

Mark 8:14–30; Matthew 16:16–18

We're going to look at St. Mark's Gospel again in the eighth chapter, and I would like you to go to verse 14. This is something that we need to look at today especially, because we don't understand sometimes what's going on.

"The disciples had forgotten to take any food with them and they had only one loaf with them in the boat." One loaf of bread. You have to remember here that just that very day or afternoon or morning, the Lord had fed four thousand people with the second miracle where He multiplied the bread and multiplied the fish. And so, the disciples come along with one loaf of bread in the boat, and Scripture says, "Then He gave them this warning, 'Keep your eyes open; be on your guard against the yeast of the Pharisees and the yeast of Herod'" (Mark 8:15). Now, let's look at that. What is Jesus telling them? What's He telling you and me? This book was not just for the apostles. This is not a rendition of what Jesus said to His apostles only; it's what Jesus said to every man, woman, and child in this whole wide world. And what is it?

"Beware!" He says. "Keep your eyes open; be on your guard against the yeast of the Pharisees and the yeast of Herod." Are we on our guard today? Are our eyes open to bad yeast? What is yeast? What does it do? Well, take flour, water, eggs, put yeast in it, put it in a nice warm place, and it starts getting big. Give it a little punch, it goes down, and then all of a sudden it begins to rise again to make bread.

So, what makes it do that? It's the yeast. There's a power in the yeast. It makes something small into something larger. So, when Jesus said beware of the yeast of the Pharisees and Herod, He meant their example. Their example was worldly: ambition, wealth, glory—human glory; their example was hypocrisy, where they said one thing and they did something entirely different. Their example was jealousy and hatred. And so, He said, "Beware! Look. See. Keep your eyes open!"

You know, I think if we kept our eyes open today, a lot of our teenagers and young adults would never fall. You cannot have a teacher or any religious or anybody tell you that premarital sex is okay. Keep your eyes open! That's bad yeast! Herod was living with his brother's wife, and the Pharisees were just hypocrites, putting burdens on people. But they didn't carry them themselves. Jesus said to watch out for those kinds of people.

Today, we use misdirected compassion, commonly known as peer pressure, as if that's an excuse. We're not keeping our eyes open when we see bad fruit! You see what happens to people who smoke a carton of cigarettes every three to four days. You see what happens when a person drinks and drinks and drinks. You're not blind. You see what happens when people indulge in sex to the point where they just have no return. You see what happens!

He says, "Keep your eyes open! Look at the yeast around you."

Well, these poor apostles, Lord, they never caught on. I don't think we do either. Scripture says here, "And they said to one another, 'It is because we have no bread'" (Mark 8:16). They never caught on. They said, "What's He talking about? It is because we have no bread." You know, sometimes these apostles are absolutely amazing. But then we look at ourselves, and we have more than the apostles had. You say, "Oh, we don't have more." Yes, we have almost two thousand years of truth, miracles, holy men and women, doctrines, dogmas, and morality. We've got so much more, and we're no more aware, our eyes are as closed as these apostles' were.

And do you want to know what the Lord thinks when we close our eyes to bad yeast? You want to know what He said? Jesus knew what they were thinking. They were so mundane and so human, and so kind of out of it sometimes. He said to them, "Why are you talking about having no bread? Do you not yet understand?" (Mark 8:17).

You know, you just see the frustration in Jesus. You know, we kind of think that Jesus is like a big statue up in Heaven with no feelings, with no care. And so you can just go around and sin all you want. Or the Father is some doting old man who is going to forgive you time and time and time again, so you can sin all you want, and it's okay.

Yeah, He will forgive you time and time again, but you've got to have effort and purpose of amendment. And so you can see the impatience and frustration in Jesus. And He says, "Have you no perception?" He's astounded at these apostles when He said, "Keep your eyes open; be on your guard against the yeast of the Pharisees and the yeast of Herod." "Are your minds closed?" He said. "Have you eyes that do not see, ears that do not hear?" (Mark 8:17–18).

You know, I can't help but think that Jesus is saying the same thing today. Broken families because of adultery, broken families because of drunkenness, broken families because of drug addiction, AIDS, gonorrhea, syphilis. And what He says here again, "Are your minds closed? Have you eyes that do not see and ears that do not hear? Or do you not remember?"

Do you not remember? You know, it's amazing to me that this generation, I think, especially, are going headlong, laughing, gleefully downhill. They all say, "Come on, Mother, you're a little bit sour tonight!" I wish that's all it was. I wish that I was just being a little negative. I wish it weren't true that our eyes are closed and that our ears are closed and that we have no perception and that we don't see and that we don't stay away from the Pharisees and the Herods in this world—the ones who preach false doctrines to you, the ones who preach false morals in life or terrible immorality and permissiveness, putting it in ads, and unbelievable things. And the Lord has to say to us, "Are you without perception? Don't you see how bad this is? Don't you see you're destroying yourselves?"

Well, it says, "When I broke the five loaves among the five thousand, how many baskets full of scraps did you collect?" (Mark 8:19). It looks as if He finally gives in, you know. And they're worried about not having enough bread. They missed the whole point of Jesus' warning against "the yeast of the Pharisees and the yeast of Herod." And so, He has to come back to their small minds, because they're so worried about their food. And you can almost feel His fatigue.

"'How many baskets full of scraps did you collect?' They answered, 'Twelve.' 'And when I broke the seven loaves for the four thousand, how many baskets full of scraps did you collect?' And they answered, 'Seven.' Then he said to them, 'Are you still without perception?'" (Mark 8:19–21). It's a very sad thing, this whole paragraph, very sad, in today's world, where everything goes, where people have really misdirected compassion. If someone should say to us, as Jesus said to His apostles, "Are you without perception?" "Don't you understand?" "Are your minds closed?" we're almost insulted. We think, "Oh, how judgmental!" "You're making people feel guilty." We're not making people feel guilty, because there's good guilt and there's bad guilt. The Lord wasn't making His apostles feel guilty; He was correcting them. If a person corrects you, it's because he loves you. There is love in correction, because He intimated here that their minds were beginning to be closed.

It's like a door shuts on you—and that's what's so amazing to me: that we would prefer the door to be shut.

And, you know, you've got those game shows where they have these three doors and you choose one. What happens? What do you think would happen if somebody had kind of X-ray eyes and could see all the wonderful things behind this one door and could see very, very bad things behind this other door? Which one would you choose? Well, you would say, "I would choose the one with all the good things." But we don't do that. We don't always do that, especially on a spiritual level. We listen to ourselves, we listen to the world, we listen to false doctrines and false concepts, as I said a minute ago. And as a result, the Lord keeps giving us inspiration and giving us all this, and we don't listen.

And so, you see here—if you've ever gotten discouraged over the whole thing—you see the apostles themselves really didn't quite understand either. So what are we saying? What we're saying is that the apostles have the same weaknesses, the same lack of comprehension, the same lack of perception as you and I have. What made the difference? What made them so enlightened? What made these men so brave? What made these men so sure of what they believe? Well, it was after the Resurrection and after Pentecost, it was the Spirit Who came upon them, and that's what we need today. We need the Spirit. We need to ask for the Spirit.

If you look at the things of God and the ways of God and the demands of God or the demands of Scripture, the demands of the Church, the precepts of the Church, the doctrines and dogmas of the Church, or whatever comes from the Magisterium, and you say, "I find this very hard, I find this very difficult, I can't accept it," then ask the Spirit. That's His role. He is the sanctifying Lord; He is the enlightening Lord. And you see these apostles here, when the Lord is accusing them of all these terrible things and they were so dull with it, and still they were vessels ready by the very fact that they were all these things, by the very fact they didn't perceive. They were in great need, and so Jesus sent His Spirit.

What a wondrous gift from God, and we can say, "Spirit, come into my heart. Holy Spirit, teach me how to pray. Holy Spirit, teach me to understand this mystery; teach me how to be aware of the presence of Jesus in my life." That's what we need to do, because it is the Spirit's role, and it takes time even when the Spirit gives you grace. It takes faith and hope and love, and especially hope. In our age, we need a lot of hope. It is to be assured that Jesus is helping me now and He's going to continue helping me on the way to Heaven, and if you want to learn a very, very beautiful little example of this, we're going to go on to Mark 8:22–26.

"They came to Bethsaida, and some people brought to Him a blind man whom they begged Him to touch. He took the blind man by the hand and led him outside the village." Jesus didn't want to heal him there with all those people. And what happens? He put spittle on the man's eyes and laid His hands on him. Now, I want you to see what He did. "He said, 'Can you see anything?' The man, who was beginning to see, replied, 'I can see people; they look like trees to me, but they are walking about.' Then He laid His hands on the man's eyes again and he saw clearly; he was cured, and he could see everything plainly and distinctly" (Mark 8:22–25).

Why did Jesus do that? He healed a leper at the snap of a finger, and leprosy is something else. He was increasing this man's faith. See how gentle Jesus is? See how He waits for us in our slowness of mind? Don't get discouraged. Don't say, "Well, holy is not for me, it's all for these intellectuals or philosophers or theologians. I'm just a housewife. I'm just a workingman. I'm just a student." But you're not just anything: you're a child of God, and Jesus is willing to wait. How patient of Jesus.

See, the blind man didn't ask to be healed. Scripture says the people brought him, probably dragging him there, and said, "Please, we beg You, Jesus, heal this man." The Lord took him by the hand. So, this blind man didn't say, "Lord, that I may see." Jesus is so wonderful! He put spittle on His finger, and He rubbed the man's eyes. He says, "What do you see?" "Something like trees." And He put His hands on him again. Jesus didn't lose power. He could have healed him right off the bat, but the man had to build up his faith and build up his hope.

"And Jesus sent him home, saying, 'Do not even go into the village'" (Mark 8:26). Notice how Our Lord is always saying to the people He healed, "Don't tell anybody. Don't tell anybody. Just go show yourself to the priest. Acknowledge your gift before God." Why? Because He knew every time He healed somebody or every time He raised somebody from the dead, they were after Him. They were going to kill Him, but He would not be killed until His time had come, until His hour had come. One time, when the Pharisees tried to dissuade Jesus from going to Jerusalem, they said, "Go away. Leave this place, because Herod means to kill you." And do you remember what Jesus said? "You may go and give that fox this message: Learn that today and tomorrow I cast out devils and on the third day attain my end" (Luke 13:31–32). And then, not before then, would they hurt or harm Jesus. There was a time.

And you and I sometimes wait too long. Don't wait any longer. Why don't you just kneel or sit down and go over your life with Jesus? Oh, I don't mean pick it apart. Just say, "Jesus, Lord, I don't even know if You're listening." We know He is, but maybe in your heart you don't have that faith yet. "So, Jesus, I want faith, and I want hope. I want to believe, I want to know, and I want to love. I want to love. And I've got all these problems, Lord, and I don't know what to do with them. I don't know how to solve them. So give me light."

That's how you talk to Jesus. It's wonderful to say formal prayers. But you have here apostles who didn't understand, who were, as Our Lord said, "without perception." You have a blind man here who was dragged probably by his relatives for Jesus to heal him, and he had to be healed slowly. Because you see, Jesus is very interested, not only in these physical things you need or material things you need, but in your soul. His main interest is your soul. We go after everything *but* our soul.

So the Lord is not going to heal the blind man physically unless He was sure this man had the faith to continue knowing, loving, and serving God. Because in His mind, there is one thing necessary. And that one thing necessary is eternal salvation, which He paid for and offers you. You've got to accept. You have to accept. And I suppose one of our biggest problems is this one, the very next verse, Mark 8:27, "Jesus and His disciples left for the villages around Caesarea Philippi." And He put the question to them. "Who do people say I am?" And they said, "Oh, John the Baptist," and another said, "I heard someone say this morning you were Elijah." I'm adding a few things here. And one said, "Ah, I heard somebody else yesterday say they were sure you were one of the great prophets."

It wasn't what He wanted to hear. Well, He said, "And who do you say I am?"

Peter spoke up. He said, "You are the Christ" (Mark 8:29). And in Matthew and Luke, it has more to this passage. Matthew 16:16–18 says, "You are the Son of the living God." And Jesus says, "Blessed art thou, Simon Bar-Jona: because flesh and blood hath not revealed it to thee, but my Father who is in heaven. And I say to thee: That thou art Peter; and upon this rock I will build my church."

And so, we see here something for our spiritual lives. We are without perception, but Jesus waits for us and helps us build our faith. But at the very end, we need to know, we need to believe that Jesus Christ is the Son of God, Lord of Lords and King of Kings! He is your Master. He is your Teacher. He is your Savior.

Remember, His Mercy endures forever.

13

The Gratitude of the Leper

Luke 17:11–19

During our Scripture study, we're going to look at something that we've heard a hundred times. We have heard this particular story in the Gospel as many times as we've gone to church, at least once a year and perhaps more. And if you are a Scripture reader, then you have really grasped it more than that.

And it's thanksgiving. And you say, "Well, I know about Thanksgiving. It's a feast day." Well, it is once a year in this country. But do you realize how little you thank people? You know, one of the greatest things in the world, next to love, is gratitude. In fact, for the person who loves, it's impossible not to be grateful, because gratitude is an element of humility. Did you know that? Proud people are never grateful.

Did you ever do something for somebody who is kind of arrogant? Did they ever say thank you? No! Why? Because, as far as they're concerned, they deserve it; there's nothing you can do for them that they don't deserve. In other words, it's your bounden duty to do it for them.

Some of you wives have never heard a thank-you from your husbands. They come home, you have a beautiful meal on the table, everything is beautifully clean, and they never say, "Well, thank you, sweetheart." Nothing! They're the breadwinners. They expect you to put the bread on the table. They expect you to keep the house clean. If you don't, they'll grumble.

Oh, we're great grumblers—grumble, grumble, grumble, grumble. We're negative. There is so much negativism in the world! And we're negative very easily. It's always easier to be obnoxious than it is to be good. Now, we don't like to admit that. We like to think that goodness comes natural to us. It does not come natural to us. And so, some of you husbands never thank your wives for the pie she made that you like or the roast she made the way you like it. You just take it for granted. "She's my wife. I own it, she bakes it."

If you've got that attitude, I would think you would have one miserable existence. And yet according to the statistics in St. Luke's Gospel, we're talking about maybe 90 percent of the people never say "thank you." And you know, I know that for a fact, because we get mail every day. We get petitions, petitions, petitions, petitions, petitions. And it's very seldom that somebody will say, "Thank You, Lord." or "Dear sisters, thank the Lord for all He has done for me." Not that you don't need things, but you know, God is not there like one of these vending machines you put a quarter or forty cents in and you get a Coke or you get a hot dog. He's not a machine. The Lord is a Being. He is a Person, a Person Who loves, a Person Who wants to hear "thank you."

But if you don't have a humble heart, you're not going to ever say "thank you," either to your children, your husband, your wife, or your friends. Christmastime comes along, and you almost know the gift you're going to get from Aunt Mary—a tie or a towel. And as she's handing you the present, you thank her for the towel before you even open it, but it's a halfhearted thing. We don't have *guts* gratitude. You know what guts gratitude is? Well, it comes from the heart and says, "Thank you so much!" We never say it that way.

Well, the Lord had the same problems that maybe you have. And you know one thing about lack of gratitude? You just don't feel like doing anything anymore. It does not encourage you to virtue. Well, let's look and see. I want you to turn to Luke 17:11.

"Now on the way to Jerusalem He travelled along the border between Samaria and Galilee. As he entered one of the villages, ten lepers came to meet him" (vv. 11–12). Well, you and I—at least I know for myself—have probably never seen a leper. I have never seen a leper—never. I've seen pictures. It must be a very disheartening sight. Your heart has to go out to these people who are so bereft. Their fingers fall off, and it's just a terrible thing. And here are ten of them. They know Jesus is coming. They've heard about Him, and they want to be healed. They're tired of being outcasts.

"They stood some way off." Why? Because they couldn't get near people. If they did, everybody would run away, screaming, and they would be considered unclean. They couldn't go to the Temple to worship. It was a big thing. And they used to have little bells, and if you heard that bell, you looked around. And if they weren't at a great distance, then you created the distance. You have to get that mentality in your mind. And it says, "They stood some way off and called to him" (vv. 12–13).

See, they didn't come up to Him and say, "Jesus, look at my hands. Heal me." They called at a very great distance and said, "Jesus! Master! Take pity on us." I mean, they were the worst. They called Him "Jesus," which means "Savior." They called Him "Master," which was Lord, and they said, "Take pity on us." They were humble. "Look at us! We're dying. We're rotting away. Have pity on us."

Well, the Lord never moved. He didn't say, "Come here; I'm going to touch you." He didn't say, "I will come to you." Nothing! He said, "Go and show yourselves to the priests" (v. 14). Now, why would He say that? Because if you were a leper and you were registered as one, that means you were kind of excommunicated. You could not enter, and you couldn't even get near the Temple. Now, if for some reason you were healed of your leprosy, you had to go to the priests, show them you were healed, and prove you no longer had leprosy; then you got reinstated into the synagogue and the Temple services.

The marvelous thing about Jesus is that He didn't say, "I'll heal you." He asked the lepers to go and do what they would do if they were already healed. And this is very important, because it says here, "Now as they were going away they were cleansed" (v. 14). They were cleansed at this point! See, it wasn't that Jesus said, "Be cleansed," and all of a sudden, all this new skin and new fingers and new eyes were formed. He said, "Go and show yourselves to the priests," which means they had to do the last thing first. So even before they were healed, Jesus said, "Go and show yourselves to the priests."

They were on their way. They were obedient. So, first they were humble; they acknowledged Him as Lord, and now they were obedient. They all turned toward the Temple. "Now as they were going away they were cleansed," which means all of a sudden they're walking down the road, and one notices, "Look, your fingers are new. They've got new skin!" And the other one would say, "Look, you're not limping!" As they went, they were cleansed.

So, their obedience paid off. There wasn't one of those ten who stood there and said, "Wait a minute. How am I going to show myself to the priests? I'm still a leper; I'm not healed."

Well, you see, that would have been the commonsense thing to do. But immediately, they turned around as lepers and went on their way to the Temple to show themselves, and on their way, they were cleansed.

"Finding himself cured, one of them turned back" (v. 15). Maybe he was halfway to the Temple, and he looked at himself and said,

"Lord, look! I've got real fingers again!" Now, we see something entirely different from the other nine. All ten were humble about it; all ten called Him "Lord"—"Master." And all ten turned around; they were obedient. They turned around and they went toward the Temple, even before they were healed. So, I don't think at that point we could say they had faith. They had faith in Jesus. But only one had some other ingredient.

Now, most of us would've been satisfied with their faith. Most of us would have been satisfied that we had turned around, we believed Him, and we went, and that's it. Most of us would've been satisfied that we were obedient and had shown ourselves to the priests. Now one was "praising God at the top of his voice" (v. 15). I mean, all the way back from the middle of the road, before he even reached the Temple, he's hopping and skipping and praising God and yelling and singing. And when he finds Jesus, what does he do? He throws himself at the feet of Jesus and thanks Him! "Thank You, Jesus! Thank You, Lord!" It was an enthusiastic thank-you because Scripture says he was "praising God at the top of his voice."

Now, there's a little rub in here. Of the ten lepers, nine were Jews, and one was a Samaritan, which is another word for heretic—one of these people who doesn't believe what you believe and doesn't accept the full truth. They may have a half-truth. And so, what happens to that? Well, first you become prejudiced, then you become kind of haughty because you have it all and they only have a part, and then you become hateful, which means, "Get out of my way. I don't want to speak to you. I don't want to talk to you. I don't want anything to do with you." That's really what prejudice is.

Some of you have had prejudice since you were children, because your family had it. And if I were to ask you, "Why don't you like the yellow race, the red race, the black race, or whatever religion? Why don't you like Catholics? Why do you persecute them?

Why don't you like Baptists or Methodists or Presbyterians?" most couldn't even answer me why. It's because you heard somebody say something about them and you believed it. So, the best way to handle a lot of things for some people is just to hate everybody, and you don't have to worry about anybody.

Well, a Samaritan was that type of person. He suffered; he was the one who was affected by all the negative and very hateful words of the Jews. The Israelites hated the Samaritans. In fact, if you touched a Samaritan or did anything for a Samaritan, you were declared unclean; you associated with heretics.

Now, Our Dear Lord said something here. He put a little dig in the people in the crowd. Because what He said to them, "The only one who came back was the Samaritan, the very person you hate. The very type of people that you say are not following the law of God or the Temple regulations or all the rules the Pharisees put upon those people—the very one, this one person." And the Lord was always using these heretics as an example—the Samaritan who took care of the man that fell by robbers. He was a Samaritan!

Well, that really made it hard for the Jews to listen. And one of the things about the Lord is He really didn't care how hard it was for you to listen; He meant to tell you the truth. We don't want to hear the truth today. We are not interested in truth. We're only interested in our own little opinions. Now, for most of you, the nine who walked their way didn't do anything wrong, for they did what the Lord told them to do: "Go and show yourselves to the priests."

Well, what is there to do? What's wrong with that? But God wants you and me to go that extra mile. And that extra mile was to turn around and walk back, praising God all the way. And it said, "This made Jesus say, 'Were not all ten made clean? The other nine, where are they?'" (v. 17).

Now, there are no indications in the Scriptures that the other nine ever came back. There are no indications in the Scriptures that they were healed or not healed. But the Lord says here, "Were not all ten made clean?" So they were definitely healed. We don't know if the leprosy came back; I doubt it. "Were not all ten made clean?" So they probably went to the Temple, showed themselves to the priests, got reinstated, and then dropped Jesus like a hot potato!

And you know, as ungrateful as you probably feel this is, you and I do the same thing. We sure do. We're constantly asking God for things, and as soon as we get them, we forget about Who gave them to us. Oh, we even make vows. I mean, we can really put on a big act.

You know, when you get in a lightning storm or you get yourself in a foxhole, you make all these great promises. "Lord, if I get out of this jam, I'm going to do all these things. I'm going to say a Rosary every day, I'm going to be good, and I'm going to Mass every Sunday." These are the things you should do anyway. What's the big deal? Nothing big. Why do we keep promising what we're supposed to be doing already? You say, "Well, I'm going to do this, Lord. If You heal me, if You cure me, if You get me out of this predicament, I promise You I'll go to Mass every Sunday."

You've *got* to go to Mass every Sunday. You're *supposed* to go to Mass every Sunday. You're *supposed* to give God honor and glory every week. Well, some of us make pretty big sacrifices. Some of us promise big things like, "I'm going to say a Rosary every day for the next year. I'm going to fast every Friday for the next year. I'm going to do this; I'm going to do that." But when you have been cleansed and when you have gotten exactly what you wanted, you forget. You don't keep your promise. You don't even say, "Thank You, Jesus."

If you have made a big promise to the Lord, the next time you get to Confession, tell Father you never kept that promise, and see if he can't give you something else to do. Because you see, then you lie to God, and that is not a good thing to do. And I would not make a vow. I would be very careful. You don't need to make promises to God to get what you want. But if you do, maybe God will inspire you, and maybe it's the only way to get you to Mass on Sunday. But if you make a promise, keep it! Keep it! Don't treat God like you do your neighbor.

You say, "Well, you're trying to put the fear of the Lord in me." That's exactly what I'm doing, and I hope I succeed, because it wouldn't hurt any of you to get a little bit of the fear of the Lord.

Scripture continues, "It seems that no one has come back to give praise to God except this foreigner" (v. 18). See, the Israelites had all the light; the Samaritans had a part of it. They were considered heretics, foreigners, and aliens. They had their own temple, their own everything. Well, what really bothered the Lord is that the children who were given so much were not grateful.

You know, this country is in that position. I really do feel that way. I think this country in general has gone out to people and done a lot of things. That does not give them a license to do what they're doing. A country that has abortion as a law is in bad shape, and they probably don't even understand it or know, and that's the pity of it all — when we're in bad shape and don't know it; when our minds and our hearts are so mixed up, that we cannot judge truth from error or light from darkness. When we get to that point, that's what's so sad here, you see: the ones who had the full light and knew that they must praise God and thank God. I can't imagine having such a terrible disease and not going back to the One Who heals you. This is beyond me.

But something happens to us along the way. You say, "Hey, look. I deserve to be like everybody else. I deserve all my fingers on my hands. I deserve all of this, so why should I be grateful?" See, there's an element to gratitude that is consistent humility. So now we see what was wrong with them. They were obedient, but it was for a selfish motive. They think, "Well, if I go, something good will happen to me, and it did!" They were humble. Was it from their heart or was it because they were in such dire straits? They were in dire straits, so they could say, "Jesus, Master." They were the lowest of the low. Everything was up from there on.

So, were they really humble when they said, "Jesus! Master! Take pity on us?" Or was it because they realized their state? Where was their humility? Was it human humility or supernatural humility? Well, when we learn the fruits of their obedience and humility, we know they were on the surface. Jesus was not their Lord, or they would have come back! They were obedient only because there was nothing else for them to do. They had tried everything, and they were the lowest of the low. Why not take a chance? What's there to lose? So, now, what seemed to be humility and obedience was not. What proved that? Gratitude.

Gratitude proved the source. This man who came back was humble in his heart, not just in his mind. He was humble in his heart. He was obedient in his heart. "I will do anything for this man they call Jesus." Well, you see, that's why Jesus said to him, "Stand up," because he had thrust himself before the Lord, "and go on your way. Your faith has saved you" (v. 19).

Now, you see the other nine just did it because that's the thing you do to get this healing, and that's all they wanted. There was no real, sincere humility or obedience or belief that Jesus was Lord. "He was some kind of prophet, and He did a big thing, and I'm going my way. I'm going to live my life"—selfish, self-oriented, egotistical. It was a fake obedience and a fake humility.

Let's ask ourselves today, "Do I really have faith in Jesus, or am I willing to do anything just to get what I want?" If I'm willing to do anything just to get what I want, then I will not be saved, because I don't have the heart. So, be grateful. Say before you retire this evening, "Jesus, I need You. I love You, and I'm so grateful."

14

The Witness of John the Baptist

John 1:19–34

In our Scripture, we're going to look at someone who's not really too popular. I like the kind of people who aren't too popular, because they must have a real important message, or they'd be more popular. The people today that are very, very popular usually tell you what you want to hear.

Now, there are some people in the Scriptures who never said anything anywhere near what the people wanted to hear. With some people, they were very popular, because they didn't like the way things were going. Like today, if you're a conservative and you "rah, rah conservatism" in front of liberals, the liberals hate you, but conservatives think you are terrific, and vice versa. So, we all have itchy ears—that's what the Lord calls it. He says people have itchy ears. What does that mean? Well, it means that you hear only what you want to hear. And if someone says something about sin, for example, you don't want to hear that! You want to do what you want, when you want, how you want, and you don't want anybody to "bother your conscience" or make you feel guilty.

But see, if a prophet of God comes along and says the truth, sometimes it does make you feel guilty. Why? Because you're not adhering to the truth — it's that simple. It's really not complicated. Maybe you're in sin; maybe you're committing sin. But we don't even like to hear the word "sin"! In some of the catechesis, some of your CCD classes, some of your parishes, nobody says "sin."

Well, somebody has to say it, because you could go to Hell! And that's eternal. Somebody doesn't say this is what God wills from you and this is what He objects to; that's what the Church is for. Now, you can run around and finally find some church that will let you do about anything, all in the name of Jesus! But you know, you can kill your conscience! You can get to the place where your conscience doesn't bother you at all, because it's dead.

So you know, if you think I'm trying to be a wet blanket, you're right! I think we all need a little wet blanket every once in a while. We need somebody to shock us back to reality, and that's exactly what the person I'm going to talk about did. That was John the Baptist. Not popular. A few what they would call fanatics in those days loved him, because he gave it to Herod. He gave it to Herodius. He gave it to the Pharisees, the Sadducees, and the doctors of law. He let them have it day after day, day after day, one after another. He never stopped. And he was a man who was raised in the desert. You know, he was the son of Zechariah and Elizabeth, raised in the desert on locusts and wild honey. That isn't a lot. He didn't have to worry about overeating or too many calories. So, he must have been a kind of tall, scrawny-looking man who wore sheep wool and lived in a cave. And he'd come out every so often and blast everybody who had walked in.

You know, that isn't a way to win friends and influence people. So I wonder today if we don't need another John the Baptist. We need somebody who is willing to come out of the cave with God's knowledge and grace and sit down with us and say, "Look, sweetheart, you're on the wrong path, and if you don't get on the right path, you're going all the way downhill."

So, we're going to look at it. I want you to open up your Bible to John 1:19, which says, "This is how John appeared as a witness."

Now, you know, sometimes, we think a witness is always the person who says, "Jesus loves you." When he's speaking of truth and if his life depicts that truth, then he is a witness. But if he tells you one thing and he lives another thing, he's not a witness. He's just a bigmouth, but he's not a witness. A witness means somebody sees in you something that you may have said or will say. He sees it before he hears it. And I wonder if that's not one of our problems today, that we don't have enough witnesses to various truths and various areas of the Lord's life. So, it said, "This is how John appeared as a witness. When the Jews sent priests and Levites from Jerusalem to ask him, 'Who are you?'"

Well, you can't blame them for that. All of a sudden, they hear about this scrawny-looking man who seemingly is a prophet, and he's in the desert, and he's sometimes wading in the waters of the Jordan, and he's yelling and screaming, and he's saying, "You brood of vipers!" And that's all right.

They said, "Hey, who are you who can do this stuff?" But "he not only declared, but he declared quite openly, 'I am not the Christ'" (v. 20). See, they all knew somebody was coming. They all knew somebody was on the way!

"'Well, then,' they asked, 'are you Elijah?'" Now, you say, "Do they believe in reincarnation?" No. They knew from the Scriptures that Elijah was supposed to come in the last days and live among us and die as all men die. So, they thought, "Well, are you the Elijah who's supposed to come back?"

"'I am not,' he said" (v. 21). You know, some people would like other people to believe they're more important than they really are. John was not that way. He was a prophet of truth, and he spoke the truth, whether it was about Jesus, the Lord, the Father, the Scriptures, or himself. His truth went through his entire life.

It would've been nice to say he was something more, which was certainly a temptation, because he was very popular among the people.

"Are you the messenger? Are you the Christ? Are you the Savior?"

He could have said, "Yeah, I'm pretty good." But he was humble, and he said, "No, I'm not the Christ, and I'm not Elijah."

So then they began to say, "Well, who are you?" You see, we all want to be sure that the truth we hear is given to us by someone who has been sent! And you know, I don't know for sure, but I think sometimes that's why we don't listen. Maybe we're not sure that the people we listen to have been sent to us by God. Maybe their lives are not what they should be, so we just get a little mixed up and say, "Wait a minute! Who sent you?"

And so, these people are asking the same question, and John is forthright. He says, "No, I'm not Christ. I'm not the Elijah."

"Are you the Prophet?" Now, what does that mean? Well, many of the Jews expected someone to come in the caliber of Moses, someone who would create great things and do great prodigies and separate the Red Sea again and go in there and conquer Rome and deliver the people. I mean, he would be a military man, a man of great power. And they called him "the Prophet."

So they said, "Are you the Prophet?" John answered, "No" (v. 22). I imagine by this time, they're getting frustrated. He's not the Christ. He's not Elijah. He's not the great Prophet they've been waiting for.

"Who are you?" Look, these are soldiers. They said, "We must take back an answer to those who sent us. What have you to say about yourself?" (v. 22). By what authority do You baptize, for example? You know, up until that time, baptism was not something popular. It wasn't even something you had done to you. You stand in some water, and they dunk you. That was the baptism of repentance; that was not the baptism of Jesus. So John said again, the truth: "I am, as Isaiah prophesized."

The Witness of John the Baptist

So, he puts himself right smack in the Scriptures. See, they suspected he was someone special, *very* special. But they missed the boat. He was not in the Scriptures as Elijah was or Moses or even the Messiah. He said, "I am, as Isaiah prophesied: *a voice that cries in the wilderness: 'Make a straight way for the Lord'*" (v. 23).

Well, there aren't too many of us who want to be the voice of one crying in the wilderness. We just don't. We want to be a voice among many voices. Why? Because we want to be sure we're going to be popular, and whatever we say is going to be popular, and whatever we say is going to be accepted, and we want to be sure we've been sent by God. We want to do all of these things. We are not a people who are willing to be a voice in the wilderness!

If you were willing to be a voice in the wilderness in your office or the place you work where everybody's telling filthy jokes all day long, believe me, that is a wilderness! Why are you afraid, then, to stand alone? Do you think it's easy to be a Christian? Do you think it's easy to stand, saying, "I am the voice of one crying in the wilderness"? There is *nothing* in wilderness!

Have you ever been to the desert? When I go back and forth to California, I look at that desert for miles and miles and miles, and there's nothing but sand and mountains, some are snowcapped. You go a long time before you find the little village somewhere. It's wilderness.

But today, you live in a wilderness in your neighborhood. You may have houses on every side. But if they're all the kind of people who are worldly and greedy and promiscuous and who care for nothing and no one, and neither God nor man do they fear, you're living in a wilderness. Maybe your home is a wilderness. You can't talk about Jesus, because your husband has a fit, your kids think you're nuts, and vice versa. It's amazing to me how many women will not speak about the Lord, and their husbands are all caught up in the Lord. You've got a desert in your own home!

Living the Scriptures

But John was not afraid to be that one voice. You know, I am convinced that if every Catholic were willing to be that one voice, if every Christian were willing to be that one voice, this whole wide world would change, and it would change overnight! But we don't want that! We don't want to feel alone. You know, in the desert, you don't even hear your own echo. I mean, that's how alone you are. You get up in the mountains, and you can yell and scream, and you get this echo that comes back. But in the desert, there's nothing. It's hot all day and freezing all night. So, that's what you call being alone.

But John wanted everybody to know exactly what Isaiah said he would be, "a voice that cries in the wilderness." If Jesus needs you, He needs you to be that one voice in the wilderness. And as long as you laugh at these filthy jokes in your office, then your coworkers are going to keep telling them. As long as you listen, there's going to be someone there who has a mouth like a garbage can.

But you're afraid. You don't want to be a voice in the wilderness. But then you'll never be a John the Baptist, and you're going to have to account for that one day.

The people around you take the name of Jesus in vain. I don't know how they do that. Is their vocabulary so small, that the only name they can use is the name of God, and they use it as a curse word, not a word of blessing? Well, you might be that voice in the wilderness that says, "Wait a minute. Look, I don't like to hear that." And if you're stuck, and there's nothing you can do about it, then every time you hear a curse word or the Lord's name taken in vain, mentally say, "Jesus, I love You. Jesus, I'm sorry. Jesus, I ask pardon for this person."

Make up for it. That's really being a voice in the wilderness.

But why are you a voice in the wilderness? Tell me, what is the fruit of standing tall when everybody around you is crumbling? To make straight the way of the Lord.

See, there's fruit from that. Somebody in your office—maybe you won't touch them all—but somebody somewhere is going to be touched by your perseverance, your love, your determination, and your witness. Look, don't worry about the opinions of men. Jesus said one day, "As for human approval, this means nothing to me" (John 5:41).

Well, I wish that were true with the rest of us. The opinions of men mean so much to us that we will not only change our opinion: we'll change our lives, our morals, and everything else, because we don't want to be a voice in the wilderness.

I feel like a voice in the wilderness. I'm the only one talking, it seems to me, about chastisement. Everybody else is saying there's going to be peace and love and love and peace. Well, the only way we're going to get love and peace is when the Lord cleans house.

Scripture continues, "Now these men had been sent by the Pharisees, and they put this further question to him, 'Why are you baptizing if you are not the Christ, and not Elijah, and not the prophet?'" (vv. 24–25). I mean, "What right do you have?"

Now, does John defend Himself? You and I would have said, "I have every right! I am the one whom Isaiah prophesized, and I have even the right to baptize." He never even seemingly answered them. What he did say was, "Look, if you find fault with me, you wait till the One Who comes after me arrives."

That's really not an answer to the question! But John is constantly telling the truth. He says, "I baptize with water." He didn't say why, and he didn't say anything about his authority. He says, "Put all that jealous, petty stuff aside." He wasn't going to get involved in the pettiness of other people's minds. "But there stands among you"—that means right now—"unknown to you"—now, that must have really got them thinking; in other words, "If you think you're having trouble with me, there is Someone standing around here you're *really* going to have trouble with—"the One who is coming after me; and I am not fit to undo His sandal strap" (vv. 26–27).

Now, maybe that doesn't mean anything to you. But you have to realize that this was a decadent society, a society that was full of immorality, and it was terrible. And the chief priests were not much better—they were scheming politicians. In the midst of all that, John the Baptist stood out like a light. He was penitential, he was God-fearing, he was everything a Jew should be and more! He was without human respect. But he says, "Don't look at me. There's One among you that I am not worthy to unloose the straps of His sandals."

And this was at Bethany. Well, that kept them quiet. Because now they've got their mind off John, and they're wondering, "Who is He? Who is this Man he speaks of? Is He in our midst now?" You know, Jesus is in your midst a lot. And I bet if I came to your parish and somebody said, "I wish I could see Jesus," and I said, "Look around. He's in your midst now!" you'd think I was having a vision. But He *is* there.

Well, the next day, seeing Jesus coming toward him, John said, "Look, there is the Lamb of God that takes away the sins of the world" (v. 29). You and I say it at every Mass.

"This is the one I spoke of when I said: 'A man is coming after me who ranks before me because he existed before me'" (v. 30). He didn't say, "He was born before me" but that "He *existed* before me." There he's talking about the eternity of the Son of God, and they missed it.

He said, "'I did not know him myself, and yet it was to reveal him to Israel that I came baptizing with water.' John also declared, 'I saw the Spirit coming down on him from heaven like a dove and resting on him. I did not know him myself, but he who sent me to baptize with water had said to me, 'The man on whom you see the Spirit come down and rest is the one who is going to baptize with the Holy Spirit'" (vv. 31–33).

The Witness of John the Baptist

See, John said, "I did not know him myself." Why? He was in the desert. Tradition has it that when John was born, the Pharisees at the time got a kind of hint that this man was very special, a precursor of the Messiah, and they persecuted his father. And so, Elizabeth and John had to escape into the desert. And that's where he was raised, and that's where he grew up, in the desert. But when it was time, the Lord said to him, "The One on Whom I rest, that is the One. That's the One whom you're announcing."

"Yes, I have seen and I am the witness that he is the chosen one of God" (v. 34).

You know, all these people, these new theologians, these new Scripture scholars say Jesus didn't know Who He was. I just don't understand how you can say that. John knew Who He was. Mary knew Who He was. So did the shepherds and the three Wise Men. What is it? Is Jesus the only one in the dark? Why do you have to twist everything and warp people's minds so that the Gospel seems to them something unreal? I wouldn't want to be you when you enter the Kingdom, for having warped people's minds by this kind of crazy interpretation of Scripture.

"I have seen Him," says St. John. "I am the witness. I say to you, he is the chosen one."

We have a lot of saviors going around, a lot of messiahs. "Don't believe them," the Lord said. "And they will say, 'Here he is and there he is'" (see Mark 13:21–22). And Jesus said, "Do not believe them."

All you New Agers out there, going around worshipping some kind of stupid crystal, and you Catholics running around looking for the union and brotherhood of man: *You look for Jesus! That's Who you should look for!* And then men will love one another. You are not the Messiah! You are not God! And there is no other God but the Lord God and His Son, Jesus. If John the Baptist were here today, he would verbally rip you apart. Because he said, "I have seen the Chosen One of God. There is no other."

And don't pay any attention to those who promise you the world, because, believe me, that's all they can promise you. They can never promise you eternity. Only Jesus can prepare that mansion for you in eternity. There is no other. Only Jesus is Savior. Only Jesus is Messiah. Only Jesus is Lord. Only Jesus prepares a place for you. "I am going now to prepare a place for you" (John 14:2).

Every century does not have its own Savior. The world has only one Savior. And John the Baptist, I think, speaks today in the Church that says, "Christ has died, Christ is risen, and Christ will come again." We say that over and over and over. So, I think it would be good if you and I were John the Baptist to our neighbor and proclaim as he did: "Jesus Christ is Lord."

15

St. John the Baptist's Commitment to Truth

John 3:22–36

We're going to continue with John the Baptist. We talked about his witness and how he said he was not the Christ. He wasn't going to pretend to be somebody he wasn't, which is something we do all the time today. Everybody has this kind of pretend person who they are, especially those who are name-droppers.

Have you ever seen a name-dropper? The first time they see you or they meet you, they say, "Oh, I know So-and-so!" Well, who cares? You can stand on your own. We do have a tendency to want to pretend to be somebody we're not, to possess things we don't possess. We're in this kind of mode of pretense.

Well, John the Baptist wasn't. And so he explains it to everybody. And then Jesus is in their midst, and He begins. He chooses His apostles. There's the great miracle at Cana, when Jesus changes water into wine as a prefiguring of changing wine into His Blood.

Well, there are now two men, one a precursor announcing, witnessing to the One Who is to come, and the One Whom John the Baptist spoke of and said, "There stands among you the one who is coming after me; and I am not fit to undo his sandal strap" (John 1:27).

Living the Scriptures

Well, Jesus has spoken now to Nicodemus one night. You know, he's the man who couldn't understand what it meant to be born again. And he asked a foolish question, "How can a grown man be born? Can he go back into his mother's womb and be born again?" And Jesus said, "You, a teacher in Israel, and you do not know these things!" (John 3:10).

Well, it's after all of that and more. And Jesus, right before the Passover, goes up to Jerusalem. And in the Temple, He found people selling cattle, sheep, and pigeons, and moneychangers. Now, all of these were legitimate businesses, setting up their counters. But they weren't supposed to be in the Temple. You had to buy these things there if you wanted to sacrifice to the Lord. But now you see, they started here and they are coming closer and closer until the Temple itself is of no value to them. The awe has gone. The awesomeness of nearing the presence of God has gone. It's big business. "We got to get closer to where the people are."

Well, we all know what happened. We all know that Jesus got extremely angry. And He said He would destroy this Temple. Jesus now is almost doing what John the Baptist did. Do you remember what John the Baptist did? "You brood of vipers!" he said, and he goes out and tells Herod and Herodias, "It's not lawful for you to live together. You've taken your brother's wife! It's against the law!" And he just raves and raves.

Now, we see Jesus cleansing the Temple of the moneychangers, of all the people in there who were greedy and had no desire for God. Well, after all that, we see Jesus working now. We see Jesus becoming more and more visible. And we see John now fading into the background, just as it should be.

"After this, Jesus went with his disciples into the Judean countryside and stayed with them there and baptised. At the same time John was baptising" (John 3:22–23). So there was a point when Jesus was baptizing and John was baptizing.

St. John the Baptist's Commitment to Truth

"Now some of John's disciples had opened a discussion with a Jew about purification, so they went to John and said, 'Rabbi, the man who was with you on the far side of the Jordan, the man to whom you bore witness, is baptising now; and everyone is going to him" (John 3:25–26). Now, you know, that's an amazing statement. Why? Because they knew. John said, "This is the one." They heard the Father's voice. They knew this was the Anointed One of God, and yet they clung to their own little group. They weren't broad enough to say, "If this is the Man John bore witness to, if this is the Man of Whom John said, 'There stands among you ... One Who is going to baptize with the Holy Spirit,' then everyone should go to Him."

Well, it's amazing to me that they were jealous. You know, I find that in the Church. It's amazing. You find pro-life groups quarreling among themselves. You find people devoted to Our Lady who have all kinds of organizations, and they quarrel with each other about who's doing this and who's doing that. And you just want to say, "Hey, everybody! Get your act together, will you?"

Keep your eyes on Jesus. Don't worry about your little John the Baptists running around. They're only vehicles God uses to get you to Him! You've got to put aside the vehicle. You're not supposed to have devotion to founders or foundresses. That's unhealthy competition. You're supposed to have devotion to the Lord, Whom these founders and foundresses follow. Every organization that is spiritual in nature or moral in nature that is leading the people to God ought to embrace every other religion, every other organization, especially those in the same Church.

What's the difference if you belong to a Marian Center, a Legion of Mary, or a sodality? What is all this bickering? What is all this frustration? What is all this mountain climbing that you do? Are you there for a position? So, you're president of the sodality. Lord save us, who cares? Who cares? There's somebody in the world who knows you're president of your sodality. It's an office, it's a job. The importance is Jesus Christ, the Lord, and Mary, His Mother.

You know, if every Catholic organization ever got its act to-gether and really respected and loved and worked together with every other organization, we'd have a renewed Church! But we're all like John the Baptist's disciples. They were jealous. They said, "Look, Master, this Man is also baptizing. Now, what?" As if it took something away from John. John has served his purpose. It's time to go. "John replied: 'A man can lay claim only to what is given him from heaven'" (v. 27).

Ah, he answered. He answered. I am convinced, if all the pro-life groups got together and worked for a common cause, instead of everybody in his own little niche, it would be a tremendous force. And John said, "You yourselves can bear me out: I said: I myself am not the Christ; I am the one who has been sent in front of Him. The bride is only for the bridegroom; and yet the bridegroom's friend, who stands there and listens, is glad when he hears the bridegroom's voice" (28–29).

You know, you can't even imagine the utter unselfishness of St. John the Baptist. He had one thing on his mind. He was single-minded. "Blessed are the pure in heart," and that's what it means. The Lord said in the Beatitudes, "Blessed are the pure in heart, for they shall see God" (Matt. 5:8). Well, John the Baptist was pure in heart. He had a single mind. He didn't care anything about himself, and he didn't care anything about anybody else. I don't mean he was indifferent. I mean he wasn't tied down by people's opinion of him to push him forward.

And he said, "No, no, no! I am a precursor. I am the one who announces Him. I do not take His place." Then he said, "The bride is only for the bridegroom; and yet the bridegroom's friend, who stands there and listens, is glad when he hears the bridegroom's voice. This same joy I feel, and now it is complete" (v. 39). He was happy when he knew that the mission of Jesus was beginning to take root. His disciples were jealous because they had themselves in mind. They were in their own little famous niche. They wanted to be admired by the people. They wanted to be the disciples of the great prophet. Suddenly, they see someone getting more attention, someone else getting more popular, being more loved by the people. You see, that's the essence of jealousy. It seeks self above all things and everyone. And John explained to him, "Wait a minute."

You know, it's an amazing phenomenon, but very often men and women who are married get along well together until a child comes along. And the child is the fruit of their love and is supposed to bring them closer together. Sometimes, the wife gets jealous or the husband gets jealous. The child gets too much attention. They are spending too much time with the child. Parents get this way, because they don't have the spirit of John the Baptist. They're not saying, "He must increase, and I must decrease."

And John goes on and he says, "He must grow greater, I must grow smaller." He knew his role, and he never veered from it. "He Who comes from above is above all others." He's greater than I am. "He who is born of the earth is earthly himself and speaks in an earthly way. He who comes from heaven bears witness to the things he has seen and heard" (vv. 30–31). There he's talking about the divinity of Jesus. He said, "I am of earth." John the Baptist was the last prophet. "I only speak of earthly things. But the one who is sent from heaven can speak of what he has seen and heard. I cannot speak of what I have seen and heard. I do not come from the Father. I come from earth. My mother was Elizabeth; my father, Zechariah. I am of this world. The bridegroom comes from the Father, and He's the One you must go to. I am only preparing the way."

"Even if his testimony is not accepted; though all who do accept his testimony are attesting the truthfulness of God, since he whom God has sent speaks God's own words" (vv. 32–33). He is really setting his disciples straight. He says, "Jesus comes from heaven, and He has been sent to you. And whatever Jesus says, you must listen to, because those very words come from God."

How many of you listen to the Bible? How many of you read this Gospel? How many of you know what's in it? Some Bibles have all the words of Jesus in red, so you can pick them up faster. I find red a little hard to read, but it's a good idea. If you just went to the Scripture and sometimes picked out what Jesus said, do you live by that? That's what John the Baptist said. "Don't go by the world. Don't go by what this one says or that one says. Go by Jesus! He is the One you're sure was sent by God! And then he goes on. He says, "God gives him the Spirit without reserve" (vv. 34).

This is John the Baptist speaking! "The Father gives Jesus His Spirit without reserve. So, don't go around looking for another Messiah. There are no other Messiahs. You follow the enemy. You are being deceived by the enemy, who promises you everything of this world. And do you see how John the Baptist knows he's of earth and he's willing to give it up? He knows Jesus is of Heaven, and he says, "Listen to Him. He's got the Word. He *is* the Word. The Father sends Him, and He's got the Spirit without reserve. He is the fullness of the Spirit, and the Father loves the Son and has entrusted everything to Him."

Oh, the knowledge that John the Baptist had! That knowledge is phenomenal. Here's a man who said not long ago, "I don't know Him," and then suddenly he sees Him. And he has to keep coming back and telling his disciples, "The One I saw, the One I witnessed to." And now, he describes Jesus fully. And you have to know that Jesus and John must've spoken into the night at some time or another. They must have known each other in some way, maybe unknown to their disciples. They must've spoken. No one could tell John the Baptist all of this except God Himself—no one. You see, where there is truth, there is no jealousy.

St. John the Baptist's Commitment to Truth

I don't know about you, but I think jealousy is one of the worst evils in the world. It has been the cause of murder and evil things — anger, hatred, greed. And it's all because we try to put ourselves above someone and we feel unloved. We feel others are unjust. We feel others are depriving us of something if they give something to someone else. And it's all me, myself, and I. And we begin to hate. We begin to be suspicious. We begin to be covetous.

That's what these disciples were doing with John, they were coveting their great prophet. They wanted to protect him from this other popular Man. But John has said, "He's the Bridegroom. I'm only the Bridegroom's friend." And he goes on, "Anyone who believes in the Son has eternal life." That's John saying this. "But anyone who refuses to believe in the Son will never see life: the anger of God stays on him" (v. 36).

You know, if you're having a problem with faith — and today I don't question that some of you do, because nothing seems to be stable in so many areas. You read one catechism, and it says this. You read another catechism, and it says that. You do this, you do that, and you get all kinds of feedback. You read papers from theologians, you read magazines and newspapers, and everything contradicts the other.

Whom do you believe? And John the Baptist has the answer. He's got it right here in John 3:27–36. If you're having problems with faith, I would read this once a day. Why? Because I think by reading it, you will understand Who Jesus Christ, the Son of God, is. If you're a New Ager and you're having problems and you're asking some piece of crystal to direct your life, you're really in trouble. All you stargazers who run around spending hundreds to thousands of dollars trying to figure out what star is influencing your life today — nothing God has created influences your life! Only God influences your life! Get that through your head. No star and no group of stars even knows you exist. It is the Lord God Who directs your life. He is the One Who loves you. He is One Who created you before time began. He is the One Who sent His Son to live and to die for you. No star decided whether you're going to have a good day or a bad day! You make choices in favor of Jesus, and then you have a good day or a bad day. That's something between you and God. You are not a victim of gravity. You're a child of God. And that's why I say you must read St. John's Gospel and read it over and over.

"Even if His testimony is not accepted, it is nonetheless true." You are the one who will suffer if you don't accept the testimony of Jesus, that He is sent by God. It says here, "Anyone who believes in the Son has eternal life, but anyone who refuses to believe in the Son will never see life." Well, John the Baptist is talking about Heaven. Whoever refuses to believe in the Son will never see Heaven. And the anger of God stays on him—that's Hell—because he has made a choice—a bad choice; nonetheless, we make choices. John was not going to fall into the pit of wanting to please people.

I know some of you ministers and priests really advise people to do sinful things just to please them. You don't say what the Church teaches, because you're afraid. Why don't you read about John the Baptist? Why don't you ask the Lord to give you the courage to stand alone if you have to, but to tell the truth with love and compassion? Because if you as a teacher have itching ears, if you want to hear only what you want to hear, and you put aside everything else, you can imagine what those who listen to you will have. John the Baptist was not going to do that. He was not going to fall into the pit of pride and lies. He wanted the truth. He wanted to know. And he explained to his disciples, "I am the Bridegroom's friend. I am not the Bridegroom. I am not the One Who was sent to you. I am only the one to prepare the way."

All mountains will be made low and all valleys raised high. That's what you should be, because I believe that Jesus will come again. Oh, I'm not talking about the Second Coming. God comes in every century in different ways to help His people, to convert His people. I believe the Immaculate Heart of Mary will triumph, and I believe, and I will say it over, on December 8, 1988, began the conversion of Russia through a horrible earthquake. But at least it brought people together of every nation. It exposed the hearts of people who said, "I will help even one who does not believe what I believe or even one who has persecuted me or hates me."

My friends, we live in serious times. We live in times of great grace and the power of the Spirit and the power of Mary's Immaculate Heart. Her Heart will triumph. She has promised this act at Fátima. The Lord God will work through His Mother, and Russia one day will be converted, and we will have a time of peace. But before that happens, there will be chaos. But you and I in the midst of it all must and should have peace and joy in our hearts.

16

The Raising of Lazarus

John 11:1–44

We call the Bible "Living Scripture," because that's exactly what the Scriptures are supposed to be to you in your life, and that's what they are. To the Lord God, everything in this book is present; it isn't past; it isn't like a history book. In history, everything is past to us. In the eyes of God, everything is now. There is no past with God, and there is no future; it's all present—now.

So, when you read the Scripture, Jesus is speaking to you, He speaks to me. And every event in His life, every parable, everything He said, everything He did, everything that was done to Him by others is all a part of our daily lives. We all have our birth, we all are born again, we all are living a passion, we all have an agony sometimes, we all have people nail us to the cross, nail you against the wall. There are times when you live and die over and over and over again through tragedy, through heartache, sometimes through despair.

And then that glorious day we call death, when we see Him face-to-face, is a kind of resurrection for us before the general resurrection. And what I mean by that is that when the soul sees God for the first time face-to-face, then that is the Glorious. Now, you know, whether we take a little detour or not is something else. But all in all, we do go through the Passion of Jesus, through the life of Jesus in our own lives, perhaps not exactly, but the spirit, the heartache, and the soul of it is in us, as it was in Him.

And so, today we're going to look at the eleventh chapter of St. John, and we're talking here about the resurrection of Lazarus. Before Jesus went through His Passion, He performed the miracle of miracles. Now, you wonder what made this different. After all, He did raise the son of the widow of Nain. They were carrying him out on a stretcher, and Jesus saw the widow crying, and He said, "Don't cry." And He raised Jairus's daughter from the dead. This was not the first time Jesus raised someone from the dead.

But this is different. And both times, the dead had just died. I mean, it was a matter of hours, perhaps. Now, this is quite different. I mean, this man Lazarus is buried. And we're going to see exactly what happens and how we can apply this to our daily lives.

It said, "There was a man named Lazarus who lived in the village of Bethany with the two sisters, Mary and Martha, and he was ill. It was the same Mary, the sister of the sick man Lazarus, who anointed the Lord with ointment and wiped his feet with her hair" (vv. 1–2).

You remember how Jesus was in the house of the Pharisee, and the Pharisee said to himself, "If this man were a prophet, he would know who this woman is that is touching him and what a bad name she has" (Luke 7:39). And Jesus went on and really straightened out the Pharisee. He said, "She was forgiven much, and that's why she loved much."

"The sisters sent this message to Jesus" (John 11:3). Jesus was their friend, and He loved them. That means they had a kind of special, special friendship. And John 11:5 says, "Jesus loved Martha and her sister and Lazarus." They were family. "Yet when He heard that Lazarus was ill he stayed where he was for two more days." Now, if you're a good friend of someone, especially if you have the power to heal, and all of a sudden you find out that friend is sick unto death, well now, that's something different. This is something you want to take care of immediately. If someone's in an accident, you don't wait two days before you go and see that person, especially if it's a loved one. You rush to the hospital. But Scripture is very specific here that Jesus stayed away two more days "before saying to the disciples, 'Let us go to Judaea'" (vv. 6–7).

He knew it, but He's trying to prove something. There was a real message. And you know, a lot of times, we don't understand God's plan in our lives, and we wonder why is He waiting? Why couldn't I get this two days before? Why couldn't I have gotten this last year? And we don't understand that there is a purpose to every delay. There's a purpose to every no in our lives and every yes in our lives, for every petition that's granted, every petition that is not granted.

And so Jesus waits. He just kind of walks around, stays with the crowd, talks to them. And it says here that the disciples got a little bit excited, because they said, "Rabbi, it is not long since the Jews wanted to stone you; are you going back again?" (v. 8).

Jesus says something kind of strange. You know, sometimes it seems like Jesus doesn't answer the question, but sometimes the answer is really the answer we need rather than the answer to the question we asked. And Jesus said, "Are there not twelve hours in the day? A man can walk in the daytime without stumbling because he has the light of the world to see by; but if he walks at night he stumbles because there is no light to guide him" (vv. 9–10). What does that mean? You know, so many of us today walk in darkness. And I think the bad thing about it is that we don't even know we're stumbling. We don't even know we're on the wrong path. And if someone tells us so, we're incensed, we're angry. We get a real persecution complex.

And Jesus says, "You've got to walk while it's day." While you have time, you must think and pray and get close to Jesus, especially during these times. These are serious times we live in, serious times. Because the Lord God's effort to straighten everything out in this world, there's going to be a lot of pain and tragedy and confusion. But it's the only way to push back the darkness so you no longer stumble. And He said, "Our friend Lazarus is resting. I am going to wake him" (v. 11).

You know, it's strange how the Lord talked about death. He never considered the death of the body as death. Whenever He said So-and-so is dead, that meant So-and-so lost his soul. The only kind of death that Jesus speaks about is a loss of the soul. To Him, Lazarus is resting.

And the apostles said, "Lord, if he is able to rest he is sure to get better" (v. 12). They never, never caught on to the real meaning of what Jesus said. And you know why? They didn't think. They didn't meditate. They didn't really look and kind of ponder, as Our Lady did, what Our Lord is saying. They heard it, they made a rash judgment, and they went on. And that's why so much of it never sunk in their hearts and in their minds.

"The phrase Jesus used referred to the death of Lazarus, but they thought that by 'rest' he meant 'sleep'" (v. 13). The physical death, the Lord always considered sleeping. Why? Because the soul never, never dies. The soul never dies! The only death Jesus talked about is when the soul loses itself in Hell. It loses God. It says to God, "I don't want You. I don't need You. I don't want to live with You forever." *That's* death!

And then Jesus put it plainly, "Lazarus is dead" (v. 14). They didn't understand yet. Being with Jesus for three years, and they didn't understand that the only death is when you die spiritually. And you know, some people walking around look healthy and robust, and they're at all these spas and they do all these exercises, yet their souls are dead! Their bodies are living, but their souls are dead! They live in sin. They tempt God. They do all kinds of terrible things—satanic worship and worldliness. Ach! They're really dead inside. And what's walking around is just a kind of—I don't know what it is—like one of these models you see in store windows. I bumped into one the other day. I said, "Excuse me," and it was one of these fake models just standing there. But it looked so real, I thought it was a person. That's how some people walk around. They look beautiful on the outside, but inside are dead men's bones.

Well, "Lazarus is dead; and for your sake I am glad I was not there because now you will believe" (vv. 14–15). Now, we got the reason why He stayed two extra days.

"Then Thomas—known as the Twin—said to the other disciples, 'Let us go too, and die with him'" (v. 16). Oh, what a statement! None of them died with Him. They all ran, except John. And I firmly believe if he had not stayed so close to Our Lady, he wouldn't have fared much better.

"On arriving, Jesus found that Lazarus had been in the tomb for four days already. Bethany is only about two miles from Jerusalem, and many Jews had come to Martha and Mary to sympathize with them over their brother. When Martha heard that Jesus had come she went to meet him. Mary remained sitting in the house" (vv. 17–20).

But Mary was angry. You know, it's not like Mary to just sit there. "Mary remained sitting in the house." She was hurt. She couldn't believe that Jesus would stay away that long when her brother was ill and would let him die! She couldn't believe it.

Martha, now, is not one for greeting. She also was hurt. As soon as she met the Lord, she didn't say, "Hello, Lord," or kneel at His feet and say, "Lord, I'm so sorry You weren't here." No, she corrects Him! She said, "'If you had been here, my brother would not have died, but I know that, even now, whenever you ask of God, he will grant you.' 'Your brother,' said Jesus to her, 'will rise again'" (vv. 21–23).

Living the Scriptures

Now, here's Martha the theologian coming along. She wants Him to know how much she's learned and how smart she is. And she says, "I know he will rise again at the resurrection on the last day" (v. 24). So, what's new? I mean, little Martha is just kind of bold. First, she corrects Him, and then she corrects Him again in telling Him, "Look, I know that. Now, what are you telling me?"

You know, Jesus is so patient with us when we get so smart-alecky. "Jesus said, 'I am the resurrection. If anyone believes in me, even though he dies he will live'" (v. 25). See, the connection? Your mother, your father, and everyone you know and love may have died, but Jesus said, "They live." Why do we mourn so much? Oh, I know we mourn loss, and it is a grieving period, and there's nothing you can do about that, and it's okay to grieve. We grieve for ourselves. But there is no death.

Jesus said that "even though he dies"—where the body is not operative anymore—"he will live, and whoever lives and believes in me will never die" (vv. 25–26).

Do you see? He's talking about the immortality of the soul. That's what's so important—the immortality of the soul. You know, it's important for you and me to understand that when we take such good care of our bodies, which is fine, we must not push aside our souls. You can't just say, "Well, I'm going to take care of my body" and then never read Scripture, never go to Mass, never go to church.

Now, before we go on, I think we'll just give you a little time to think about that. How much care do you take of your soul, which is going to last forever, which never dies? That's what the Lord said! Now, if you're concentrating entirely on the body—all its pleasure, everything you can give it, everything you can do for it or to it—and you ignore the soul, you see, there's such an imbalance. And that's how sometimes people think they're doing great, because they "feel good." That means they're in good health. But what is the health of our souls?

The Raising of Lazarus

Our Lord asked, "Do you believe this?" It's important that you believe that you have an immortal soul that never dies and that you must care for it, because your body begins to wear down like a car: your hair gets grayer, you get more wrinkles, you can't hear right, this happens, that happens, your feet begin to hurt where they never hurt before. But your soul is alive and vibrant — and never, never, never, never, never dies.

"'Yes, Lord,' Martha said, 'I believe that you are the Christ, the Son of God, the one who was to come into this world'" (v. 27). What kind of answer is that? The correct answer, because only God, only the Son of God, could tell you that you have an immortal soul that will never die and that it shall rise again!

Well, Martha goes and runs. She kind of suspects something might happen, and she runs to get her sister. And she says, "The Master is here and wants to see you." Well, Mary is such a loving individual. She gets up and she runs to Jesus and she says exactly the same thing her sister said. "Lord, if you had been here, my brother would not have died" (vv. 28, 32). And she was crying, I mean, the tears were flowing down her eyes.

But you see, you have to realize, too, that they had professional mourners. I mean, you hired these people to come and wail and cry at your funeral. And they came with her. So, you had all these wailers and people crying. They didn't particularly love Lazarus or even perhaps know him. That was their job.

"At the sight of her tears, and those of the Jews who followed her, Jesus said in great distress with a sigh that came straight from the heart ..." (v. 33). This was a deep, heavy sigh, meaning, "Oh, I'm sorry. I'm sorry." But then He wept. It says there, "Jesus wept" (v. 35). He cried. He cried over Martha and Mary's tragedy.

Now, you know, if you were the Lord and you knew that this man was not going to be there very long, and you were going to raise him from the dead, why would you cry? Why wouldn't you or some of you charismatics have said, "Look, why don't you have more faith? I'll raise him up. Don't cry." And people are scandalized when they see somebody crying at a funeral. They think, "Well, you ought to whoopee-do it" over somebody who has died. "It's four days now; it's not like he just died."

But we don't have a heart when we say things like that. Jesus wept, because He saw the sorrow of somebody He loved—Martha and Mary—and He cried with them, regardless of what He was going to do for them. At that moment, Jesus was a Man who lived in the present moment. That particular moment called for compassion. It's like going into a hospital and somebody is in great pain, maybe after an operation, and you walk in and say, "Hey, what are you crying about? It's going to be over in two days."

That's a terrible thing to say! That's a terrible attitude to have, and when doctors and nurses have that kind of attitude, it's really bad. It doesn't matter if the patient is going to get well in three or four days or hop out of that bed. It only matters at that moment that the patient is in tears, because he has a lot of pain. And that's the lesson that Jesus taught us. Be a person of the present moment. That toothache or backache may be gone next week. That is not the point right now. Right now, it calls for your sympathy, for your compassion, and you do something about it for your neighbor.

If there's one lesson we need today, it's this one, because today we have lost compassion. We're accustomed by television, magazines, and newspapers to seeing the most atrocious murders and terrible things done to human beings in serious countries—punishments beyond the wildest imagination of torture. We're hardened. We put up a hard-coated steel over our souls, so that when these things hit us, we don't feel them. And we do it out of the excuse that, "Well, there's so much going on, I can't take it."

But Jesus took it for your sake. Well, it says, "But there were some who remarked, 'He opened the eyes of the blind, could he not have prevented this man's death?' Still sighing" — you see, Jesus was sighing because He couldn't believe the incredulity of the people — "Jesus reached the tomb.... He said, 'Take away the stone.' Martha said to him, 'Lord, by now he will smell'" (37–39).

See, always explaining everything to Jesus. "Jesus replied, 'Have I not told you that if you believe you will see the glory of God?' So they took away the stone. Then Jesus lifted up his eyes and said ... 'Lazarus, come out!'" (vv. 40–43). And suddenly, the dead man was at the entrance of this tomb, all wrapped in swaddling clothes — that's what they looked like, anyway.

Well, no matter what condition your soul is in, no matter how much you have ignored your soul and paid a lot of attention to your body, ask the Lord before you retire tonight, "Lord, raise my dead soul up. Forgive me of my sins, and say to me, 'Come forth to my love.'"

Mother M. Angelica
(1923–2016)

Mother Mary Angelica of the Annunciation was born Rita Antoinette Rizzo on April 20, 1923, in Canton, Ohio. After a difficult childhood, a healing of her recurring stomach ailment led the young Rita on a process of discernment that ended in the Poor Clares of Perpetual Adoration in Cleveland.

Thirteen years later, in 1956, Sister Angelica promised the Lord as she awaited spinal surgery that, if He would permit her to walk again, she would build Him a monastery in the South. In Irondale, Alabama, Mother Angelica's vision took form. Her distinctive approach to teaching the Faith led to parish talks, then pamphlets and books, then radio and television opportunities.

By 1980 the Sisters had converted a garage at the monastery into a rudimentary television studio. EWTN was born. Mother Angelica has been a constant presence on television in the United States and around the world for more than forty years. Innumerable conversions to the Catholic Faith have been attributed to her unique gift for presenting the gospel: joyful but resolute, calming but bracing.

Living the Scriptures

Mother Angelica spent the last years of her life cloistered in the second monastery she founded: Our Lady of the Angels in Hanceville, Alabama, where she and her Nuns dedicated themselves to prayer and adoration of Our Lord in the Most Blessed Sacrament.